PEACE INTEGRATION & HUMAN RIGHTS

Compiled from the lectures of

SHAYKH-UL-ISLAM
DR. MUHAMMAD TAHIR-UL-QADRI

MINHAJ-UL-QURAN INTERNATIONAL

Minhaj-ul-Quran International
292-296 Romford Road
Forest Gate
London E7 9HD
United Kingdom

For Sales & Distribution enquiries:
0800 047 4078
publications@muslimyouth.org.uk

Visit us on the World Wide Web at:
www.muslimyouth.org.uk

First Published July 2010

Compiled, Transcribed, & Edited by Muslim Youth League UK
Published by Minhaj-ul-Quran International (UK)

ISBN. 0955 1888 65 5

Cover Design & Typesetting by Muslim Youth League UK
Printed by Mega Basim, Istanbul, Turkey

Special thanks goes to all those who tirelessly laboured in order to manifest this work. May Allah increase you all in excellence, and May His pleasure and the pleasure of His Final Messenger ﷺ always be with you.

بِسْمِ اللَّهِ الرَّحْمَٰنِ الرَّحِيمِ

مَوْلَايَ صَلِّ وَسَلِّمْ دَائِمًا أَبَدًا
عَلَى حَبِيبِكَ خَيْرِ الْخَلْقِ كُلِّهِمِ
مُحَمَّدٌ سَيِّدُ الْكَوْنَيْنِ وَالثَّقَلَيْنِ
وَالْفَرِيْقَيْنِ مِنْ عُرْبٍ وَّمِنْ عَجَمِ

O Lord send endless blessings & peace,
Upon your beloved, the best of creation...

Muhammad, Master of both Worlds, and Both Species [human & sprite]
and both Assemblages - Arabs and all others

EXCERPT FROM IMAM BUSIRI'S RENOWNED 'POEM OF THE CLOAK'

1268 C.E

﴿صَلَّى اللهُ تَعَالَى عَلَيْهِ وَعَلَى آلِهِ وَصَحْبِهِ وَبَارَكَ وَسَلَّمَ﴾

Abundant Peace and blessings of Allah the Exalted be upon the Prophet,
his Family, and his Companions

"Spread Peace, You Will Be Secure"

Prophet Muhammad (Blessings & Peace be upon him)

Bukhari/Ahmad ibn Hanbal/ibn Hibban/Abu Ya'la

TRANSLITERATION KEY

ا	*alif*	*A*	ط	*ṭā*	*ṭ*
		ā (long vowel)			*Ṭ*
		Ā	ظ	*ẓā*	*ẓ*
ب	*bā*	*b*			*Ẓ*
ت	*tā*	*t*	ع	*'ayn*	'
ث	*thā*	*th*	غ	*ghayn*	*gh*
ج	*jīm*	*j*	ف	*fā*	*f*
ح	*ḥā*	*ḥ*	ق	*qāf*	*q*
		Ḥ	ك	*kāf*	*k*
خ	*khā*	*kh*	ل	*lām*	*l*
د	*dāl*	*d*	م	*mīm*	*m*
ذ	*dhāl*	*dh*	ن	*nūn*	*n*
ر	*rā*	*r*	هـ	*hā*	*h*
ز	*zāy*	*z*	و	*wāw*	*w* (consonantal)
س	*sīn*	*s*			*ū* (long vowel)
ش	*shīn*	*sh*			*Ū*
ص	*ṣād*	*ṣ*	ي	*yā*	*y* (consonantal)
		Ṣ			*ī* (long vowel)
ض	*ḍād*	*ḍ*			*Ī*
		Ḍ	ء	*hamza*	'

CONTENTS

PART 2
RENOUNCING TERROR, REGAINING PEACE,
AND THE FUTURE OF ISLAM

PART 3A
ISLAM, PEACE AND DEMOCRACY

PART 3B
AL-HIDAYAH EUROPE 2009:
QUESTION AND ANSWER SESSION (U.K)

EDITORS FOREWORD

YOUNG MUSLIMS IN THE WEST and in the Islamic heartlands face many questions connected to the spread of a relatively new Kharajite philosophy, which presents a half sawn-off distorted model of Islam as the representative voice. Although the current Muslim situation is full of challenges, it is also an opportunity to present Islam, with all its intellectual rigours and spiritual intricacies, to Muslims and non-Muslims alike.

This role can only be performed by an informed leadership, whose vision is multi-dimensional; rooted in the Islamic intellectual and spiritual tradition, but at the same time aware of the modern world and the spectrum of ideologies which mould it.

The present volume is a collection of transcripts from lectures delivered by Shaykh ul-Islam Dr. Muhammad Tahir ul-Qadri, an internationally renowned authority on the sciences of Islam, a former professor of law, and a close student of contemporary academia and the modern world. Whilst not delivered as a series, the themes running through all of these speeches are interrelated and particularly relevant to Western Muslims in the modern age.

In *Peace, Integration and Human rights*, Shaykh ul-Islam Dr. Muhammad Tahir ul-Qadri presents the life of the Prophet Muhammad (blessings and peace be upon him) as the ultimate model for nurturing peace and harmony in a diverse world beckoning for a solution. This unique and unprecedented lecture bridges the Prophetic example (sunnah) with the challenges faced by western Muslims living as minorities. Some of the distinguished features gleaned from the Prophet's life include: the migration to the Illuminated City of Medina; the Constitution of Medina as the first written constitution in human history; the mechanisms used by the Prophet to establish a culture of peace and security, knowledge and learning, human rights and equality, and socio-political prosperity; the historic treaty of Hudaybiyya; Women's Rights, The Prophet's governance of a multi-cultural society, and the Prophet's relations with non-Muslims.

In *Renouncing Terror Regaining Peace*, Shaykh ul-Islam begins with a linguistic and theological analysis of key tenants of Islamic faith, including Islam (Submission), Iman (Faith) and Ihsan (Excellence). Shaykh ul-Islam Dr. Muhammad Tahir ul-Qadri then eloquently describes Prophetic teachings, which uphold the principle of peace and denounce violence and terror in all their possible manifestations. The much misunderstood concept of Jihad is authoritatively unlocked, beginning with an etymological analysis of the term, followed by its implications in Islamic law. In closing, some possible root causes of extremism in the Muslim world are highlighted alongside a practical course of action anchored in the Qur'an and the Sunnah of the Prophet (blessings and peace be upon Him)

Also included in this collection is a recent *Question and Answer Session* from the UK's annual al-Hidayah Europe retreat. Questions were asked by Academics, Researchers, a Christian representative, and a Journalist. The session addresses many of the previously mentioned topics such as terrorism, integration of Muslim minorities, the West's role in ensuring a peaceful relationship with the Muslim world and more such as the misapplication of blasphemy laws in lands where Christians are minorities.

It is the sincere hope of the editors and everyone else involved in the publication of this work that the reader's understanding of Islam is deepened and rectified by this compilation. It is also hoped that this humble effort may go a long way in bringing an end to the systematic indoctrination of young Muslims here in the West and in the Muslim heartlands, as well as improving the relationship between Islam and the West.

July 2010/Rajab 1431

- PART 1 -
PEACE, INTEGRATION, AND HUMAN RIGHTS IN THE LIGHT OF QURAN AND SUNNAH

1. INTRODUCTION

LIFE TODAY IS PROFOUNDLY DIFFERENT to life in sixth century Arabia. The social, economic and political scenes have changed in manifold ways vis-à-vis the situation fourteen centuries ago. Every aspect of life, in both the individual and collective spheres has undergone radical change. Despite this then, why do Muslims the world-over continue to believe that the Prophet Muḥammad (blessings and peace be upon him) and his teachings transcend the vicissitudes of time and are adoptable in today's world. It is essential that this question be addressed in a manner that will remove the confusions of the modern Muslim, as well as provide a deepened understanding to those outside the sphere of Islām.

2. ARABIA AT THE TIME OF THE PROPHET

When one studies a personality or the teachings it propagated, it is essential that they appreciate the context and material circumstances surrounding them. Arabia, in the Prophet's time, was fraught with animosity and enmity. Decades old cycles of killings and revenge between tribes were commonplace. Society was bereft of all moral precepts, and human and social values. The whole region was engulfed by an atmosphere of violence and tyranny. Drinking was rife, women treated as sexual objects;

forced to dance naked at parties and festivals, female infanticide was an accepted norm, prejudices, bigotry and rancour had torn the fabric of society, whilst lofty virtuous traits, such as truth and generosity, benevolence and compassion were conspicuously absent. The poor and destitute were considered the bane of society and were thus publicly humiliated. Widows were considered the property of their sons and in many tribes were inherited and divided along with the other property.

3. THE PROPHETIC MOVEMENT BEGAN WITH THE REVOLUTIONARY MESSAGE OF KNOWLEDGE

The great civilisations of the Greeks, Egyptians, Indians, Romans and Persians had perished. Time had rendered their influences almost insignificant. Europe and the Christian world at large had fallen deep into the dark ages of religious wars and schism. Amidst such extreme global circumstances, the Prophetic light of Muḥammad (blessings and peace be upon him) shone forth. He was sent to an Arabia steeped in ignorance, and moral and spiritual restlessness. The Arabs to whom he was sent were illiterate, proud only of their photographic memories and their eloquence. As such, the fundamental teachings of the Prophet Muḥammad (blessings and peace be upon him) highlighted the importance of knowledge. He brought to Arabia an egalitarian civilisation and an enriched culture anchored in the word of God, the Qur'ān and his own way of the life, the Sunna.

The Prophetic movement began with the message of knowledge, education and the intimate connection of man to his Lord. The first revelation was a command to the Prophet (blessings and peace be upon him) with these words:

﴿ٱقۡرَأۡ بِٱسۡمِ رَبِّكَ ٱلَّذِى خَلَقَ ١ خَلَقَ ٱلۡإِنسَٰنَ مِنۡ عَلَقٍ
٢ ٱقۡرَأۡ وَرَبُّكَ ٱلۡأَكۡرَمُ ٣ ٱلَّذِى عَلَّمَ بِٱلۡقَلَمِ ٤ عَلَّمَ
ٱلۡإِنسَٰنَ مَا لَمۡ يَعۡلَمۡ ٥﴾

Read in the Name of your Lord, who created. He created man from a hanging mass (clinging) like a leech (in the mother's womb). Read and your Lord is Most Generous. He taught man by the pen. He taught man what he knew not.

4. THE MESSAGE OF SOCIAL JUSTICE, SOCIAL COHESION, HUMAN DIGNITY AND EQUALITY

Countering the base social behaviour prevalent in sixth century Arabia, the divine revelation expounded the dignity of the human being and his esteemed position above the rest of creation.

﴿وَلَقَدۡ كَرَّمۡنَا بَنِىٓ ءَادَمَ﴾.

And we have indeed ennobled the children of Adam.[1]

In addition to this, society and social stability were of utmost significance in the message propagated by the Prophet Muḥammad (blessings and peace be upon him). The revelations he received from God made frequent mention of justice, equity and compassion. It emphasised the importance of socio-economic justice, brotherhood and freedom. Discussing such lofty social characteristics was, to the hard-hearted Arabs of the sixth century, undoubtedly perilous, given the social and political

1 al-Qur'ān, *al-Isrā'*, 17: 70.

circumstances. However, the Qur'ānic message was instantly penetrating and persuasive, and it immediately began to supplant the destructive spiritual malaise afflicting those people. In order to eliminate bloodshed and violence, engendered by extreme rancour and hatred, the Prophet (blessings and peace be upon him) told the Arabs to purify their hearts of malice and spite, and to enter into the ocean of peace.

Barā' b. 'Azib narrates that the Prophet (blessings and peace be upon him) said:

«أَفْشُوا السَّلَامَ تَسْلَمُوا».

"Spread peace, you will be secure."[2]

4.1 THE PIONEERING NATURE OF THE PROPHETIC MESSAGE

Today such rhetoric has become commonplace and thus exhorting such values in the modern context is no great feat. However, in the hostility and turmoil of sixth century Arabia, such words were innovative. Such statements from the Prophet Muḥammad (blessings and peace be upon him) established a civilisation built on the principles of peace and love. The ḥadīth literature is replete with such sayings from the Messenger of Allāh. I will cite a few examples here, to illustrate that love, mercy and peace are the cardinal principles, in which the structure of the Islāmic civilisation is firmly rooted.

The Prophet (blessings and peace be upon him) said to his companions:

---

[2] Related by al-Bukhārī in *al-Adab al-Mufrad*, p. 179 # 362; Aḥmad b. Ḥanbal in *al-Musnad*, vol. 4, p. 286 # 18557; Ibn Ḥibbān in *al-Ṣaḥīḥ*, vol. 2, pp. 244, 245 # 491; and Abū Ya'lā in *al-Musnad*, vol. 2, p. 90 # 1687.

«وَالَّذِي نَفْسِي بِيَدِهِ! لاَ تَدْخُلُوا الْجَنَّةَ حَتَّى تُؤْمِنُوا, وَلاَ تُؤْمِنُوا حَتَّى تَحَابُّوا, أَفَلاَ أَدُلُّكُمْ عَلَى أَمْرٍ إِذَا فَعَلْتُمُوهُ تَحَابَبْتُمْ؟ أَفْشُوا السَّلاَمَ بَيْنَكُمْ».

"By Him in whose hand my life lies, you will never enter paradise until you embrace Islām and you will never become a true Muslim until you love each other. If you want to ask me how to love one another, then there is no other way except by spreading peace amongst everybody."[3]

Invoking peace upon fellow Muslims at every meeting is one of the clarion signs of Islām. It serves as a constant reminder to Muslims; that the quintessential characteristic of their way of life is peace. Not only will such conduct preserve one's religion, it will also embed in one's heart, love for fellow human beings. The narration succinctly expounds that spreading peace engenders love; love is the basis of faith and only by faith does one enter the Garden.

'Abd Allāh b. 'Amr narrates that the Prophet (blessings and peace be upon him) said:

«أُعْبُدُوا الرَّحْمَنَ, وَأَطْعِمُوا الطَّعَامَ, وَأَفْشُوا السَّلاَمَ, تَدْخُلُوا الْجَنَّةَ بِسَلاَمٍ».

"Worship the Merciful, feed the hungry, spread peace; you will (as a result) enter paradise with Salam."[4]

---

3 Related by Abū Dāwūd in *al-Sunan*, vol. 4, p. 389 # 5193; Muslim in *al-Ṣaḥīḥ*, vol. 1, p. 74 # 54; Ibn Māja in *al-Sunan*, vol. 1, p. 63 # 68 & vol. 2, p. 1217 # 3692; and al-Tirmidhī in *al-Jāmi' al-Ṣaḥīḥ*, vol. 5, p. 50 # 2688.

4 Related by al-Tirmidhī in *al-Sunan*, vol. 4, p. 253 # 1855; Ibn Māja in *al-Sunan*, vol. 4, p. 231 # 3694; Aḥmad b. Ḥanbal in *al-Musnad*, vol. 2, pp. 170, 196 # 6595, 6860; and al-Dārimī in *al-Sunan*, vol. 2, p. 648 # 2085.

In another Prophetic tradition, it is stated:

«إِنَّ السَّلَامَ اسْمٌ مِنْ أَسْمَاءِ اللهِ تَعَالَى، وَضَعَهُ اللهُ فِي الْأَرْضِ، فَأَفْشُوا السَّلَامَ بَيْنَكُمْ».

"Indeed al-Salām is a name of the Names of God, (which) Allāh has placed in the earth, so spread peace amongst one another."[5]

In yet another narration, the Prophet (blessings and peace be upon him) was asked:

أَيُّ الْإِسْلَامِ خَيْرٌ؟

"What Islāmic traits are the best?"

The Prophet (blessings and peace be upon him) replied:

«تُطْعِمُ الطَّعَامَ، وَتَقْرَأُ السَّلَامَ عَلَى مَنْ عَرَفْتَ، وَعَلَى مَنْ لَمْ تَعْرِفْ».

"Feed the people, and greet those whom you know and those whom you do not know."[6]

---

5 Related by al-Bukhārī in *al-Adab al-Mufrad*, pp. 182, 201 # 372, 426; al-Ṭabarānī in *al-Mu'jam al-Kabīr*, vol. 10, p. 182 # 10391; and al-Bayhaqī in *Shu'ab al-Īmān*, vol. 6, p. 433 # 8784.

6 Related by al-Bukhārī in *al-Ṣaḥīḥ*, vol. 5, p. 2302 # 5882; and Ibn Manda in *al-Īmān*, vol. 1, p. 453 # 357.

5. EXAMPLES OF PATIENCE, FORBEARANCE, TOLERANCE, AND FORGIVINGNESS IN THE PROPHET'S CHARACTER

As stated earlier, there are abundant narrations that illustrate the magnanimity of the Prophetic character, which not only left his Companions in awe of him, but also rendered his enemies speechless.

An example of this is recorded by al-Bukhārī in his collection and is reported by Ibn Abī Mulayka, who said:

عَنْ عَائِشَةَ رضي الله عنها: أَنَّ الْيَهُودَ أَتَوُا النَّبِيَّ صلى الله عليه وآله وسلم، فَقَالُوا: السَّامُ عَلَيْكَ. قَالَ: «وَعَلَيْكُمْ». فَقَالَتْ عَائِشَةُ: السَّامُ عَلَيْكُمْ، وَلَعَنَكُمُ اللَّهُ، وَغَضِبَ عَلَيْكُمْ. فَقَالَ رَسُولُ اللَّهِ صلى الله عليه وآله وسلم: «مَهْلاً يَا عَائِشَةُ! عَلَيْكِ بِالرِّفْقِ، وَإِيَّاكِ وَالْعُنْفَ أَوِ الْفُحْشَ». قَالَتْ: أَوَلَمْ تَسْمَعْ مَا قَالُوا؟ قَالَ: «أَوَلَمْ تَسْمَعِي مَا قُلْتُ؟ رَدَدْتُ عَلَيْهِمْ، فَيُسْتَجَابُ لِي فِيهِمْ، وَلاَ يُسْتَجَابُ لَهُمْ فِيَّ».

"Ā'isha narrates that: 'Once a group of Jews entered upon the Prophet (blessings and peace be upon him) and said: "al-sāmu 'alaykum (death be upon you)." The Prophet (blessings and peace be upon him) replied: "The same to you." But 'Ā'isha (may Allāh be well pleased with her) said: "Death be upon you and the curse and wrath of Allāh be upon you." Allāh's Messenger (blessings and peace be upon him) said: "Calm down, O 'Ā'isha! You should be lenient and merciful, and must avoid violence and obscenity." She replied: "Haven't you heard what they (the Jews) had

> *said?" Allāh's Messenger (blessings and peace be upon him) said: "Haven't you heard what I had said (to them)? I have repeated the same words, so my supplication was accepted about them and theirs about me was rejected."""*[7]

Another example of the Prophet's tolerance and magnanimity is narrated by the great Successor (al-tābi'ī) Mujāhid b. Jubayr, who said that: "A goat was slaughtered in the house of 'Abd Allāh b. 'Umar. When its meat was served to him, he inquired, 'Have you sent some meat to our Jewish neighbour? I heard the Prophet saying: "Jibrīl exhorted me to treat the neighbours well, so much so that I thought he may ask me to make them inheritors."'"[8]

The aforementioned narrations are a mere drop in the ocean of the Prophet's noble character and his sublime qualities. The reality is that the life of the Prophet (blessings and peace be upon him) is inundated with such occurrences and events. These and other such narrations establish beyond a shadow of doubt, that the Prophet (blessings and peace be upon him) set a precedent for the greatest ethical, spiritual and socio-political revolution in human history. Unfortunately, in our postmodern world of confusions and paradoxes, the Prophet Muḥammad (blessings and peace be upon him) and his enlightening message have been heinously misunderstood in the West and grossly misrepresented by the Muslim world.

There are invaluable lessons in the life of the Prophet (blessings and peace be upon him) which provide practical substantiations of the chivalrous character of the Prophet (blessings and peace be upon him). One needs only to look at and contextually understand key points in his blessed life. One such notable occasion is the emigration of the first Muslims from

---

[7] Related by al-Bukhārī in *al-Ṣaḥīḥ*, vol. 5, p. 2350 # 6038; and *al-Adab al-Mufrad*, pp. 426, 477 # 996, 1126.

[8] Related by al-Tirmidhī in *al-Jāmi' al-Ṣaḥīḥ*, vol. 4, p. 294 # 1943.

Makka to Medina. Twelve delegates from Medina, who had come to Makka during the annual pilgrimage season, pledged their allegiance to the Prophet Muḥammad (blessings and peace be upon him) and requested the Prophet to migrate to Medina. It is important to note here that before this event, the Prophet Muḥammad (blessings and peace be upon him) had lived twelve years under the sheer oppression and brutality of the Makkans. He was confined to his house, mocked in the streets of his beloved homeland and stoned by the children of Tā'if. However, when the delegates arrived from Medina, pledging their allegiance and absolute obedience to him, he did not narrate to them his story of grief and oppression. Instead he taught them seven basic principles, which, if implemented would initiate an unprecedented spiritual and social reform in the Arabian Peninsula.

He summoned them to faith in the unity of God. He then ordered them to combat social misdemeanours, prohibiting theft and adultery. He forbade female infanticide, ending centuries of oppression and injustice against women. The Prophet (blessings and peace be upon him) prohibited slander, in order to preserve the social repute of every individual, thereby preserving the sanctity of society at large. Finally, the Prophet (blessings and peace be upon him) commanded the Medinan delegates to obey him in all the good that he transmits to them.[9]

These seven principles were not only the means of social and political reform, but were also the pivot around which spiritual salvation revolved. As is evident, the primary teachings of the Holy Prophet (blessings and peace be upon him) conveyed a sense of tolerance and forgiveness to the Medinians; in an attempt to rid the society of all moral and social ills.

---

9 Ibn Hishām, *al-Sīra al-Nabawiyya*, p. 434; Ibn Sa'd, *al-Tabaqāt al-Kubrā*, vol. 1, p. 220; Ibn Kathīr, *al-Bidāya wa'alNihāya*, vol. 2, p. 526.

6. MIGRATION TO MEDINA

6.1 THE FIRST PROPHETIC SERMON IN MEDINA

Similarly, in his first sermon, upon arriving at Medina, the Prophet Muḥammad (blessings and peace be upon him) summoned the Muslims to adhere to five fundamental teachings. He said:

«أُوصِيكُمْ بِتَقْوَى اللهِ, فَإِنَّهُ خَيْرُ مَا أَوْصَى بِهِ الْمُسْلِمُ الْمُسْلِمَ, أَنْ يَحُضَّهُ عَلَى الآخِرَةِ, وَأَنْ يَأْمُرَهُ بِتَقْوَى اللهِ, فَاحْذَرُوْا مَا حَذَّرَكُمُ اللهُ مِنْ نَفْسِهِ, وَلاَ أَفْضَلَ مِنْ ذَلِكَ نَصِيْحَةً, وَلاَ أَفْضَلَ مِنْ ذَلِكَ ذِكْراً. وَإِنَّهُ تَقْوَى لِمَنْ عَمِلَ بِهِ عَلَى وَجَلٍ وَمَخَافَةً مِنْ رَبِّهِ, وَعَوْنِ صِدْقٍ عَلَى مَا تَبْتَغُوْنَ مِنْ أَمْرِ الآخِرَةِ».

"I advise you to fear God, for this is the best advice a Muslim can give another Muslim; such that he prompts him about his afterlife and orders him to fear God. Beware of what God has Himself cautioned you. And there is no advice or reminder superior to this. And indeed it is piety for one to accomplish this with apprehension and fear of his lord, and is a (means of) true assistance for what desire from the here after."[10]

«أَيُّهَا النَّاسُ! فَقَدِّمُوا لِأَنْفُسِكُمْ, تَعْلَمُنَّ وَاللهِ! لَيُصْعَقَنَّ أَحَدُكُمْ, ثُمَّ لَيَدَعَنَّ غَنَمَهُ لَيْسَ لَهَا رَاعٍ, ثُمَّ لَيَقُولَنَّ لَهُ رَبُّهُ — وَلَيْسَ لَهُ تُرْجُمَانٌ وَلاَ حَاجِبٌ يَحْجُبُهُ دُونَهُ...

---

10 Ibn Kathīr, *al-Bidāya wa al-Nihāya*, vol. 2, pp. 603, 604.

فَمَا قَدَّمْتَ لِنَفسِكَ؟ فَلَيَنْظُرَنَّ يَمِينًا وَشِمَالاً فَلاَ يَرَى شَيْئًا, ثُمَّ لَيَنْظُرَنَّ قُدَّامَهُ فَلاَ يَرَى غَيْرَ جَهَنَّمَ».

"O mankind! Advance (good deeds) for yourselves! You well know-by Allāh-which any one of you may be struck down and thus his flock will be left without a shepherd. Then his Lord will say to him, while he has neither an interpreter nor a veil, to come between them: 'What (good deeds) have you advanced for yourself?' He will look to the right and the left and see nothing. Then he will look before him and only see hell."[11]

«فَمَنِ اسْتَطَاعَ أَنْ يَّقِيَ وَجْهَهُ مِنَ النَّارِ وَلَو بِشِقِّ تَمْرَةٍ, فَلْيَفْعَلْ. وَمَنْ لَمْ يَجِدْ فَبِكَلِمَةٍ طَيِّبَةٍ، فَإِنَّ بِهَا تُجْزَى الْحَسَنَةُ عَشْرَ أَمْثَالِهَا، إِلَى سَبْعِ مِئَةِ ضِعْفٍ».

"So, whoever is able to protect his face from the fire, even by a portion of dates, let him do so. If he finds none then by a kind word for thereby one good deed is rewarded ten times it's like to seven hundred times."[12]

The aforementioned examples eliminate any misunderstanding that the West may have pertaining to the translucent teachings of the Islāmic tradition. To bracket violence and brutality with Islām is sheer injustice and is indicative of a deep rooted ignorance of its teachings. From the outset, the Prophet's message was one of love and mercy. He said:

---

11 Ibn Hishām, *al-Sīra al-Nabawiyya*, p. 496; al-Bayhaqī, *Dalā'il al-Nubuwwa*, vol. 2, p. 524; Ibn Kathīr, *al-Bidāya wa al-Nihāya*, vol. 2, p. 604.

12 Ibn Hishām, *al-Sīra al-Nabawiyya*, p. 496; al-Bayhaqī, *Dalā'il al-Nubuwwa*, vol. 2, p. 524; Ibn Kathīr, *al-Bidāya wa al-Nihāya*, vol. 2, p. 604.

«أَحِبُّوا مَا أَحَبَّ اللّٰهُ, أَحِبُّوا اللَّهَ مِنْ كُلِّ قُلُوبِكُمْ, وَلَا تَمَلُّوا كَلَامَ اللَّهِ وَذِكْرَهُ, وَلَا تَقْسُ عَنْهُ قُلُوبُكُمْ».

"Love all that Allāh loves. Love Allāh with all your heart. Do not tire of His speech and His remembrance and do not harden your hearts (by turning away) from him."[13]

6.2 THE FIRST STEP IN THE STATE OF MEDINA: ESTABLISHING INFORMAL SOCIO-ECONOMIC STABILITY

The Prophet's teachings cultivated a profound sense of mutual love amongst the Muslim community. All his noble statements and actions were redolent of the compassionate teachings of the Islāmic tradition. A beautiful illustration of this is when the Prophet Muḥammad (blessings and peace be upon him) established the pact of brotherhood between the migrants from Makka (*Muhājirūn*) and the Medinian helpers (*Anṣār*). The Holy Prophet's (blessings and peace be upon him) first step in establishing the state of Medina was not to enforce the laws of worship or institute the penal system. Rather the Prophet's priority was to establish social equilibrium, beginning with the just distribution of wealth. The act of brotherhood thus formed unwavering bonds of love and compassion between the citizens of the Medinian state, as well as engendering socio-economic stability for the Muslim.

---

[13] Ibn Hishām, *al-Sīra al-Nabawiyya*, p. 497; al-Bayhaqī, *Dalā'il al-Nubuwwa*, vol. 2, p. 525; Ibn Kathīr, *al-Bidāya wa al-Nihāya*, vol. 2, p. 605.

6.3 THE FIRST CONSTITUTION IN HUMAN HISTORY: THE CONSTITUTION OF MEDINA

The second most significant step the Prophet (blessings and peace be upon him) took upon arriving in Medina was to form a political alliance with the Jews, Christians and other non-Muslim minorities residing in Medina. A formal agreement was drafted, aimed at bringing an end to the bitter cycles of violence between the conflicting clans of Medina. The document, famously known as the Constitution of Medina, became the first written constitution in human history. In order to understand the significance of this constitution, let us take a cursory look at the development of constitutional history.

7. CONSTITUTIONAL HISTORY: A COMPARATIVE GLANCE

7.1 THE BRITISH CONSTITUTION

It is well documented that British constitutional history begins in 1100 AD with the Charter of Liberties. In 1215 King John I signed the Magna Carta, which became the first constitutional document in British history. Britain became a constitutional state with the signing of the Magna Carta and 474 years later, in 1689, the Bill of Rights was prepared. In 1701 the act of Settlement was passed followed by the Parliament Act in 1911.[14]

---

14 Knappen, M. M., Constitutional and Legal History of England, New York: Harcourt Brace, 1942; J. E. A. Jolliffe, The Constitutional History of Medieval England from the English Settlement to 1485, D. Van Nostrand Company, Inc., New York; Selected Documents of English Constitutional History, Ed. By George Burton Adams & H. Morse Stephens, London: Macmillan & Co., Ltd. 1901.

7.2 THE U.S CONSTITUTION

In 1787 America declared its separation from Britain, before which Thomas Jefferson gave the declaration of Independence in July 1776. A constitutional convention took place in 1780 followed by the Philadelphia Convention of 1787. Then the Great Compromise of American history takes place, and on the 17th of September 1787, a constitutional convention finally approved a constitution for the USA. In 1865, through the 13th amendment, they approved human rights as part of the American constitution. Then in 1920, less than a 100 years ago, through a 19th amendment, gender discrimination was removed from the constitution and women were granted the right to vote.[15]

7.3 THE MEDINAN CONSTITUTION

This brief overview of constitutional development in the West allows us to compare it with constitutional development in the Islāmic world. Issues that were settled in the West no more than a hundred years ago were well documented in the constitution of Islām by the Prophet of Islām (blessings and peace be upon him) fourteen centuries ago. In his constitution, the Prophet Muḥammad (blessings and peace be upon him) addressed his community thus:

«هَذَا كِتَابٌ مِنْ مُحَمَّدٍ النَّبِيِّ الأُمِّيِّ بَيْنَ الْمُؤْمِنِينَ وَالْمُسْلِمِينَ مِنْ قُرَيْشٍ، وَيَثْرِبَ وَمَنْ تَبِعَهُمْ، فَلَحِقَ بِهِمْ وَجَاهَدَ مَعَهُمْ أَنَّهُمْ أُمَّةٌ وَّاحِدَةٌ مِّنْ دُوْنِ النَّاسِ».

---

15 Hart, James, The American Presidency in Action 1789: A Study in Constitutional History, New York, The Macmillan Company, 1948; Melvin I. Urofsky, Paul Finkelman, A March of Liberty: A Constitutional History of the United States (two volumes), Oxford University Press, 2002.

> *"This is a constitutional document from Muḥammad, the Ummī Prophet, to all the believers and Muslims from Quraysh (who have emigrated) and Yathrab, and those (non-Muslim tribes) who follow them, joined them and will fight with them. They are all (henceforth) one community, besides the rest mankind."*[16]

A complete structure of governance was established on the basis of this constitution. Governors were appointed and power was delegated at the provincial level, forming a local government system for the first time in Medina. Political unity was created in the form of a nation-state and the Holy Prophet (blessings and peace be upon him) enforced a system based on the rule of law. One must keep in mind that this was a time when the mere word of the ruler was the law. There was no sophisticated methodology by which laws were deduced and instituted. Concepts such as consultative law, mutual assemblies, and passing resolutions (prior to the enforcement of a law) were all unheard of. These and many other political concepts were introduced to the Arabs, and by extension to the world, by the Universal Prophet (blessings and peace be upon him).

7.3.1 RELIGIOUS FREEDOM AND THE HISTORIC CONDEMNATION OF TERRORISM AND ACTS OF VIOLENCE AGAINST NON-MUSLIMS

For the first time in history a constitution declared that Muslims must coexist with non-Muslim tribes in the spirit of conviviality and mutual respect. The constitution of Medina did not sanctify war against the Jews, Christians or any other non-Muslim tribe. In fact the non-Muslims minorities were under a covenant of protection and security, such that they were allowed to retain their local customs and religious practices freely, without facing

---

16 Ibn Kathīr, *al-Bidāya wa al-Nihāya*, vol. 2, p. 620; and Abū 'Ubayd al-Qāsim b. Sallām, *Kitāb al-Amwāl*, p. 194 # 518.

antagonist reactions from the Muslims. Such actions initiated the development of a United Arabia under the banner of Islām. All this was possible as a direct result of the social and political reform instigated through the Constitution of Medina. Article sixteen of the Charter states:

«وَإِنَّ الْمُؤْمِنِيْنَ الْمُتَّقِيْنَ أَيْدِيْهِمْ عَلَى كُلِّ مَنْ بَغَى وَابْتَغَى مِنْهُمْ دَسِيْعَةَ ظُلْمٍ أَوْ إِثْمٍ, أَوْ عُدْوَانٍ أَوْ فَسَادٍ بَيْنَ الْمُؤْمِنِيْنَ, وَأَنَّ أَيْدِيَهُم عَلَيْهِ جَمِيعًا وَلَوْ كَانَ وَلَدَ أَحَدِهِمْ».

"There shall be collective resistance by the believers against any individual who rises in rebellion, attempts to acquire anything by force, violates any pledge or attempts to spread mischief amongst the believers. Such collective resistance against the perpetrator shall occur even if he is the son of anyone of them."[17]

Hence any act of terrorism or violence under the constitution would amount to a crime and was accordingly punished. The charter not only guaranteed freedom to practice religion and prohibited acts of violence, it also placed responsibility on the citizens of Medina, be they Muslims or non-Muslims, to collectively resist such acts.

Contrary to prevalent misconceptions in the West, Islām is neither an intrinsically violent religion, nor does it endorse a violent agenda. Even the most cursory perusal of early Islāmic history, specifically the Prophetic period, provide ample insight into the merciful nature of Islām, in its most pure and unadulterated form. Unfortunately, certain zealots amongst the

---

17 Abū 'Ubayd al-Qāsim b. Sallām, *Kitāb al-Amwāl*, p. 194 # 518.

Muslim community, due to their ignorance of the primary sources of the Islāmic tradition, present a narrow and utterly contorted image of this sophisticated tradition. The likes of Osama bin Laden, are neither the scholars of Islām, nor are they its true representatives; and hence they bear no authority to declare *jihād* on behalf of the Muslims. It is the duty of the majority of Muslims to shun such despotic views and proffer the true understanding of Islām, which is anchored in 1400 years of scrupulous scholarship and meticulous transmission.

8. WOMEN'S RIGHTS: A COMPARATIVE OVERVIEW

8.1 ṬĀLIBĀN DO NOT REPRESENT AN 'ISLAMIC GOVERNMENT

In addition to what has been stated thus far, another noteworthy achievement of Islām is the freedom of women. Due to the lack of access to the original sources of Islāmic Law, many estranged minds assume that Islām discriminates against women. Unfortunately, misrepresentation by self-proclaimed 'Islāmic' governments, such as the Ṭālibān, has unequivocally increased the misgivings. However, the reality is that neither the Ṭālibān, nor any other 'pseudo-Islāmic' systems for that matter, comply with the Prophetic model, implemented in the state of Medina.

8.2 WOMEN'S RIGHTS IN THE WEST

I will again provide a brief overview of the development of women's rights and the elimination of gender discrimination in the West vis-à-vis the Prophetic model. As a matter of historical fact, in the Western world, a woman was not even considered a 'legal person' until early 20th century.

Rogger Cotterrel proffers a definition of a legal person, in his work, *The Sociology of Law*, stating, "a legal person or legal subject defines who or what the law will recognise as a being capable of having rights and duties, the one who possess legal rights and duties is known to be the legal person."[18]

8.2.1 DEVELOPMENT OF WOMEN'S RIGHTS IN BRITAIN

In Britain, women began their political and social struggle to attain recognition as legal personnel and to attain the right to vote in 1897, with the formation of the National Union of Women's suffrage by Millicent Fawlett. This Union was further strengthened by the Women's Social and Political Union, established in 1903. In 1918, after immense struggle, the Representation of People Act sanctioned women over the age of 30 to vote.[19] However, this in no way eliminated gender-based discrimination, since men were allowed to vote at 21 and those in the army even younger, at 19.

8.2.2 DEVELOPMENT OF WOMEN'S RIGHTS IN THE USA

A similar account of discrimination and subsequent struggle is found in the United States of America.

The 1776 US Declaration of Independence makes no reference at all to women's rights. In fact Richard Nelson remarks that, "in colonial society a married woman had virtually no rights, the revolution did nothing to change this."[20] The same view is echoed by James Burns who asserts that the declaration refers to men, not women.[21]

---

18 Cotterrell, Roger, *The Sociology of Law*, pp. 123-124.

19 *Electioneering: A Comparative Study of Continuity and Change*, Ed. by David Butler and Austin Ranney, Oxford: Clarendon Press, 1992, p. 64.

20 Alan Brinkley, Frank Freidel, Richard Nelson Current, Harry T. Williams, *American History: A Survey*, Edition 7, New York, 1987, p. 122.

21 Jefferson, *Government by the People*, edition 15, Prentice Hall, 1993, p. 117.

The discrimination against women, was of such intensity that in 1872, Susan Anthony, the champion of women's rights activism in the US, was jailed for casting a vote in the presidential elections; since being a woman, she had no legal right to so. It was only as late as 1919 that discrimination on the basis of gender was *de jure* abolished, through the 19th constitutional amendment.

8.2.3 DEVELOPMENT OF WOMEN'S RIGHTS IN FRANCE

A similar paradigm is found in France; where, although democracy was declared in 1848, women were not allowed to vote until as late as 1944, after almost a century of suppression and struggle.

8.2.4 WOMEN'S RIGHT TO VOTE IN VARIOUS OTHER COUNTRIES

In Australia women attained the right to vote in 1921; the first lady was elected through this vote. In New Zealand, women got the right to vote in 1893; in Finland in 1906 and in Norway in 1907; in Denmark 1915, Germany 1918, Austria 1919, Canada 1919, Netherlands 1919, Belgium 1919, Switzerland 1971, Ireland, 1918, Luxemburg 1919, Spain 1931, Poland, 1918, Brazil, 1937.

The above presented examples are paradigmatic of the entire Western World. In general, women were neither recognised as legal subjects nor granted the right to vote until the late 19th or early 20th century and history is very clear about that.

8.3 WOMENS RIGHTS IN ISLAMIC LAW FOURTEEN CENTURIES AGO

Interestingly, women were declared legal personnel in Islāmic Law over fourteen centuries ago. They were given the right to vote and to partake in the political process of the day.

The Qur'ān states:

﴿يَـٰٓأَيُّهَا ٱلنَّبِىُّ إِذَا جَآءَكَ ٱلْمُؤْمِنَـٰتُ يُبَايِعْنَكَ عَلَىٰٓ أَن لَّا
يُشْرِكْنَ بِٱللَّهِ شَيْـًٔا وَلَا يَسْرِقْنَ وَلَا يَزْنِينَ وَلَا يَقْتُلْنَ
أَوْلَـٰدَهُنَّ وَلَا يَأْتِينَ بِبُهْتَـٰنٍ يَفْتَرِينَهُۥ بَيْنَ أَيْدِيهِنَّ
وَأَرْجُلِهِنَّ وَلَا يَعْصِينَكَ فِى مَعْرُوفٍ ۙ فَبَايِعْهُنَّ
وَٱسْتَغْفِرْ لَهُنَّ ٱللَّهَ ۖ إِنَّ ٱللَّهَ غَفُورٌ رَّحِيمٌ ١٢﴾

O Prophet! When the believing women appear in your presence to take the oath of allegiance that they will not set up anything as partner with Allāh and will not steal, nor will they commit adultery or kill their children or bring false blame which they have invented between their hands and feet (i.e. will not deceive their husbands declaring someone else's baby as born to her) or disobey you in what is right, then accept their allegiance and seek forgiveness for them from Allāh. Surely Allāh is Most Forgiving, Ever Merciful.[22]

While developing the structure of the Islāmic state several ladies were appointed in the Islāmic state's governmental structure. Women were appointed as members of parliament, officers and administrators in the administrative structure of the state of the Medina.

8.4 MUSLIM WOMEN HELD PROMINENT ROLES IN EARLY ISLAMIC HISTORY

One such example is that of Shifā' bint 'Abd Allāh al-'Adwiyya who was appointed as a judge of the accountability court and market administrator in the reign of the second rightly-guided caliph

22 al-Qur'ān, *al-Mumtahina*, 60: 12.

ʿUmar b. al-Khaṭṭāb (may Allāh be well pleased with him).[23] Ladies were appointed as ambassadors and as diplomats. In the tenure of the third rightly-guided caliph ʿUthmān (may Allāh be well pleased with him), Umm Kalthūm, daughter of ʿAlī b. Abī Ṭālib (may Allāh be well pleased with them) was sent in 28th AH as an ambassador to the Queen of the Roman Empire.[24] Women were given offices and responsibilities in the military services. Imam al-Bukhārī reports a narration of Anas b. Mālik about ʿĀ'isha and Umm Sulaym (may Allāh be well pleased with them) performing duties in the battle of Uḥud, in the lifetime of the Prophet (blessings and peace be upon him) himself.[25] Many other women worked as military officers in military expeditions.

Some narrations, pertinent to our disquisitions are presented below:

عَنْ أَنَسٍ رضي الله عنه يَقُولُ: دَخَلَ رَسُولُ اللَّهِ صلى الله عليه وآله وسلم عَلَى ابْنَةِ مِلْحَانَ, فَاتَّكَأَ عِنْدَهَا, ثُمَّ ضَحِكَ, فَقَالَتْ: لِمَ تَضْحَكُ يَا رَسُولَ اللَّهِ؟ فَقَالَ: «نَاسٌ مِنْ أُمَّتِي يَرْكَبُونَ الْبَحْرَ الْأَخْضَرَ فِي سَبِيلِ اللَّهِ مَثَلُهُمْ مَثَلُ الْمُلُوكِ عَلَى الْأَسِرَّةِ». فَقَالَتْ: يَا رَسُولَ اللَّهِ! ادْعُ اللَّهَ أَنْ يَجْعَلَنِي مِنْهُمْ. قَالَ: «اللَّهُمَّ اجْعَلْهَا مِنْهُمْ». ثُمَّ عَادَ, فَضَحِكَ,

---

23 Ibn Hazam, *al-Muḥallā*, vol. 9, p. 429; Ibn ʿAbd al-Barr, *al-Iistīʿāb*, vol. 4, p. 341.

24 Ibn Jarīr al-Ṭabarī, *Tārīkh al-Umam wa al-Mulūk*, vol. 2, p. 601.

25 Related by al-Bukhārī in *al-Ṣaḥīḥ*, vol. 3, pp. 1055, 1056 # 2724.

فَقَالَتْ لَهُ مِثْلَ, أَوْ مِمَّ ذَلِكَ. فَقَالَ لَهَا مِثْلَ ذَلِكَ, فَقَالَتْ: ادْعُ اللَّهَ أَنْ يَجْعَلَنِي مِنْهُمْ. قَالَ: «أَنْتِ مِنَ الْأَوَّلِينَ, وَلَسْتِ مِنَ الْآخِرِينَ». قَالَ: قَالَ أَنَسٌ: فَتَزَوَّجَتْ عُبَادَةَ بْنَ الصَّامِتِ, فَرَكِبَتِ الْبَحْرَ مَعَ بِنْتِ قَرَظَةَ, فَلَمَّا قَفَلَتْ, رَكِبَتْ دَابَّتَهَا, فَوَقَصَتْ بِهَا, فَسَقَطَتْ عَنْهَا فَمَاتَتْ.

"According to Anas b. Mālik (may Allāh be well pleased with him): 'Allāh's Messenger (blessings and peace be upon him) went to the daughter of Milhān and reclined there (and slept) and then (woke up) smiling. She asked: "O Allāh's Messenger! What makes you smile?" He replied: "(I dreamt that) some people amongst my followers were sailing on the green sea in Allāh's Cause, resembling kings on thrones." She said: "O Allāh's Messenger! Invoke Allāh to make me one of them." He said: "O Allāh! Let her be one of them." Then he (slept again and woke up and) smiled. She asked him the same question and he gave the same reply. She said: "Invoke Allāh to make me one of them." He replied: "You will be amongst the first group of them; you will not be amongst the last." Later, she married 'Ubāda b. al-Ṣāmit (may Allāh be well pleased with him) and then she sailed on the sea with Bint Qaraẓa, Mu'āwiyya's wife. On her return, she mounted her riding animal, which threw her down breaking her neck, and she died on falling down.'"[26]

Tha'laba b. Mālik (may Allāh be well pleased with him) reported:

[26] Related by al-Bukhārī in *al-Ṣaḥīḥ*, vol. 3, p. 1055 # 2722.

إِنَّ عُمَرَ بْنَ الْخَطَّابِ رضي الله عنه قَسَمَ مُرُوطًا بَيْنَ نِسَاءٍ مِنْ نِسَاءِ الْمَدِينَةِ، فَبَقِيَ مِرْطٌ جَيِّدٌ، فَقَالَ لَهُ بَعْضُ مَنْ عِنْدَهُ: يَا أَمِيرَ الْمُؤْمِنِينَ! أَعْطِ هَذَا ابْنَةَ رَسُولِ اللَّهِ صلى الله عليه وآله وسلم الَّتِي عِنْدَكَ - يُرِيدُونَ أُمَّ كُلْثُومٍ بِنْتَ عَلِيٍّ - فَقَالَ عُمَرُ: أُمُّ سَلِيطٍ أَحَقُّ، وَأُمُّ سَلِيطٍ مِنْ نِسَاءِ الْأَنْصَارِ مِمَّنْ بَايَعَ رَسُولَ اللَّهِ صلى الله عليه وآله وسلم. قَالَ عُمَرُ: فَإِنَّهَا كَانَتْ تَزْفِرُ لَنَا الْقِرَبَ يَوْمَ أُحُدٍ.

"Umar b. al-Khaṭṭāb (may Allāh be well pleased with him) distributed some garments amongst the women of Medina. One garment remained, and one of those present with him said: 'O leader of the faithful! Give this garment to your wife, the (grand) daughter of Allāh's Messenger (blessings and peace be upon him).' They meant Umm Kulthūm, the daughter of 'Alī (may Allāh be well pleased with them). 'Umar (may Allāh be well pleased with him) said: 'Umm Salīṭ (may Allāh be well pleased with her) has more right (to have it). Umm Salīṭ (may Allāh be well pleased with her) was amongst those women of Medinan Helpers who had given the pledge of allegiance to Allāh's Messenger (blessings and peace be upon him).' 'Umar (may Allāh be well pleased with him) said: 'She (ie Umm Salīṭ) used to carry the water skins for us on the day of Uḥud.'"[27]

It has been narrated on the authority of Umm 'Aṭiyya, the Ansarite (may Allāh be well pleased with her):

[27] Related by al-Bukhārī in *al-Ṣaḥīḥ*, vol. 3, p. 1056 # 2725.

غَزَوْتُ مَعَ رَسُولِ اللَّهِ ﷺ سَبْعَ غَزَوَاتٍ, أَخْلُفُهُمْ فِي رِحَالِهِمْ, فَأَصْنَعُ لَهُمُ الطَّعَامَ, وَأُدَاوِي الْجَرْحَى, وَأَقُومُ عَلَى الْمَرْضَى.

"I took part with the Messenger of Allāh (blessings and peace be upon him) in seven battles. I would stay behind in the camp of men, cook their food, treat the wounded and nurse the sick."[28]

Anas b. Mālik (may Allāh be well pleased with him) narrated:

كَانَ رَسُولُ اللَّهِ ﷺ يَغْزُو بِأُمِّ سُلَيْمٍ وَنِسْوَةٍ مِنَ الْأَنْصَارِ, لِيَسْقِينَ الْمَاءَ وَيُدَاوِينَ الْجَرْحَى.

"Allāh's Messenger (blessings and peace be upon him) went on an expedition; he took Umm Sulaym and some Ansarite women who supplied water and tended the wounded."[29]

The legal status of women was unequivocally protected in the blessed epoch of the Prophet (blessings and peace be upon him) such that if a women provided legal protection to anyone in her house, the state was obliged to respect the commitment. Zaynab (may Allāh be well pleased with her) granted protection to her husband, Abū al-'Āṣ and the state accepted this.[30] Abū Hurayra (may Allāh be well pleased with him) narrated that the Holy Prophet (blessings and peace be upon him) said:

---

28 Related by Muslim in *al-Ṣaḥīḥ*, vol. 3, p. 1447 # 1812.

29 Related by Abū Dāwūd in *al-Sunan*, vol. 2, p. 357 # 2531; al-Tirmidhī in *al-Jāmi' al-Ṣaḥīḥ*, vol. 4, p. 118 # 1575; and Ibn Ḥibbān in *al-Ṣaḥīḥ*, vol. 11, p. 26 # 4723.

30 Ibn Hishām, *al-Sīra al-Nabawiyya*, pp. 636-638.

«إِنَّ الْمَرْأَةَ لَتَأْخُذُ لِلْقَوْمِ يَعْنِي تُجِيرُ عَلَى الْمُسْلِمِينَ».

"Verily, woman can give legal protection to the whole community and that would be considered valid by the state."[31]

Another narration is reported as follows:

«إِنْ كَانَتِ الْمَرْأَةُ لَتُجِيرُ عَلَى الْمُؤْمِنِيْنَ فَيَجُوْزُ».

"If a woman would give security from the believers, it would be valid."[32]

In general, women were pivotal contributors to the formation of the Islāmic society. One of the most effective roles women fulfilled was in parliament, where female members spoke eloquently about issues confronting women specifically. A powerful illustration of this in political discourse is when 'Umar (may Allāh be well pleased with him) wished to pass a bill, to limit the amount of dowry that could be paid to a women. A female member of the parliament voiced her disagreement exclaiming, 'do you wish to limit the dowry o 'Umar, when Allāh has not.' 'Umar (may Allāh be well pleased with him) requested evidence and she responded with a verse of the Qur'ān, which states,

﴿وَإِنْ أَرَدتُّمُ ٱسْتِبْدَالَ زَوْجٍ مَّكَانَ زَوْجٍ وَءَاتَيْتُمْ إِحْدَىٰهُنَّ قِنطَارًا فَلَا تَأْخُذُوا۟ مِنْهُ شَيْـًٔا ۚ أَتَأْخُذُونَهُۥ بُهْتَـٰنًا وَإِثْمًا مُّبِينًا ﴿٢٠﴾﴾

---

31 Related by al-Tirmidhī in *al-Jāmi' al-Ṣaḥīḥ*, vol. 4, p. 120 # 1579.

32 Related by Abū Dāwūd in *al-Sunan*, vol. 3, p. 422 # 2764.

> *And if you seek to take a wife in place of another and you have given to one of them heaps of wealth, take (back) nothing of it. Do you take it (the wealth back) by means of calumny and manifest sin.*[33]

'Umar (may Allāh be well pleased with him) instantly changed his views and proclaimed that "the woman was right and the man wrong."[34]

There are abundant historical examples of this nature, which give us an insight into the political, social and legal status enjoyed by the female citizens of the Medinian state. On the contrary such rights were accorded to women in the west merely a hundred years ago, after decades of relentless struggles and suffering.

One of the greatest examples of intellectual freedom enjoyed by Muslim women is that of Lady 'Ā'isha (may Allāh be please with her), the noble wife of the Prophet (blessings and peace be upon him). Lady 'Ā'isha was a true polymath; for not only was she an exemplary Hadith master, she was also a specialist in jurisprudence, history, literature and astronomy.

Lady Sukayna, daughter of Husayn b. 'Alī (may Allāh be well pleased with them), was also an expert in literature and poetry. Hamrā' bint Ziyādat, 'Ā'isha al-Bā'ūniyya and Maymūna bint Sa'd were experts on poetry, literature and various fields of knowledge. Sayyida Shahīda, who died five years after the migration to Medina was an expert in literature and history. Fātima bint 'Alī b. Husayn was an expert in the Hanbalī legal tradition and numerous Islāmic scholars received knowledge from her. Hasan al-Baṣrī received knowledge from Rābi'a al-Qasīsa. Sharīfa Fāṭima was the governor of Yemen, Ṣan'ā' and Najrān. Shifā bint 'Abd Allāh Makhzūmiyya was a judge of the court in the days of 'Umar (may Allāh be well

33 al-Qur'ān, *al-Nisā'*, 4: 20.

34 'Abd ar-Razzāq, *al-Muṣannaf*, vol. 6, p. 180 # 10420; Shawkānī, *Nayl al-Awtār*, vol. 6, p. 314.

pleased with him). Ḥanīfa Khānūn, the niece of Sulṭān Salāḥ al-Dīn Ayyūbī, was the governor of Ḥalab.

A detailed study of the great women who played central roles in erecting the edifice of the Islāmic legal, political and spiritual edifice is outside of the scope of our disquisitions here and would require volumes.

9. MUSLIM NON-MUSLIM RELATIONS

An issue severely misunderstood in modern times is the relationship between Muslims and non-Muslims. During early Muslim rule the non-Muslims constituted a minority and Muslims were the rulers.

It is narrated that the Prophet (blessings and peace be upon him) said:

«أَلَا! مَنْ ظَلَمَ مُعَاهِدًا أَوْ انْتَقَصَهُ أَوْ كَلَّفَهُ فَوْقَ طَاقَتِهِ, أَوْ أَخَذَ مِنْهُ شَيْئًا بِغَيْرِ طِيبِ نَفْسٍ, فَأَنَا حَجِيجُهُ يَوْمَ الْقِيَامَةِ».

"Beware, if anyone wrongs someone in (a legal) contract (i.e. minorities) or diminishes his right, or burdens him (to work) beyond his capacity, or takes from him anything without his consent, I shall plead for him (against the Muslim) on the Day of Judgment."[35]

9.1 CAPITAL PUNISHMENT AWARDED TO A MUSLIM FOR MURDERING A NON-MUSLIM

'Abd al-Raḥmān b. Baylamānī (may Allāh be well pleased with him) states:

---

35 Related by Abū Dāwūd in *al-Sunan*, vol. 3, p. 108 # 3052.

أَنَّ رَجُـــلًا مِنَ الْمُسْلِمِيْنَ قَتَلَ رَجُلًا مِنْ أَهْلِ الْكِتَابِ، فَرُفِعَ إِلَى النَّبِيِّ ﷺ، فَقَالَ رَسُوْلُ اللهِ ﷺ: «أَنَا أَحَقُّ مَنْ وَفَى بِذِمَّتِهِ»، ثُمَّ أَمَرَ بِهِ فَقُتِلَ.

"On one occasion a Muslim killed one of the People of the Book (a man who was either a Jew or a Christian). The case was referred to the Prophet Muḥammad (blessings and peace be upon him). Allāh's Messenger (blessings and peace be upon him) said: 'I am most responsible to fulfil the rights of Minorities.' Then he ordered the capital punishment against the Muslim and he was killed."36

Thus the Holy Prophet (blessings and peace be upon him) declared that the blood of a Muslim and a non-Muslim had equal status.

9.2 THE PROPHET HONOURED HIS CHRISTIAN GUESTS

An example that illustrates the Prophet's kindness towards any person was on the occasion when a delegate of Christians from Negus[37] visited Allāh's Messenger (blessings and peace be upon him), and he arose to serve them. His Companions (may Allāh be well pleased with them) requested: *"let us do that for you, O Allāh's Messenger." He replied: "they honoured my Companions, and I wish to pay them back."*[38]

On another occasion the Holy Prophet (blessings and peace be upon him) allowed a delegate of Christians from Najrān to reside in his Mosque. When at the time of their worship they asked for

---

36 Set forth by al-Shāfi'ī in al-Musnad, pp. 343, 344 and al-Umm, vol. 7, p. 320; Abū Nu'aym in Musnad Abī Ḥanīfa, p. 104; al-Shaybānī in al-Mabsūṭ, vol. 4, p. 488; al-Bayhaqī in al-Sunan al-Kubrā, vol. 8, p. 30 # 15696.

37 Negus was the then king of Abyssinia.

38 Related by al-Bayhaqī in *Shu'ab al-Īmān*, vol. 6, p. 518 # 9125; and b. Kathīr in *al-Bidāya wa al-Nihāya*, vol. 2, p. 431.

permission, the Holy Prophet allowed them to worship according to their own method in the Mosque.[39]

9.3 FORGIVENESS OF THE FORMER OPPRESSORS OF MUSLIMS AT THE BLOODLESS CONQUEST OF MAKKAH

Such was the level of religious freedom granted to non-Muslims by the Prophet Muḥammad (blessings and peace be upon him). Consider for a moment the time of the conquest of Makka when the Prophet (blessings and peace be upon him) entered the Sacred City as a conqueror with an army of 10,000 men. The Makkans surrendered willingly and there was no bloodshed. However had the Prophet (blessings and peace be upon him) intended he could have sought revenge for the suffering he had endured at the hands of the Makkans. He and the early Muslims not only suffered prosecution and humiliation but several attempts were also made to assassinate him. It was in such dire circumstances that the Prophet (blessings and peace be upon him) had been forced to leave his beloved city. Upon entering Makka one Ansarite commander Sa'd b. 'Ubāda (may Allāh be well pleased with him) declared passionately: 'Today is the day of war.' The Holy Prophet (blessings and peace be upon him) expressed displeasure at this statement, took the flag from him and handed it over to his son and said to Abū Sufyān:

اَلْيَوْمُ يَوْمُ الْمَرْحَمَةِ.

"Today is the day of mercy."[40]

[39] Related by Ibn Sa'd in *al-Ṭabaqāt al-Kubrā*, vol. 1, p. 357; and b. al-Qayyim in *Zād al-Ma'ād*, vol. 3, p. 629.

[40] Related by Ibn Ḥajar al-'Asqalānī in *Fatḥu'l-Bārī*, vol. 8, pp. 8, 9; and b. 'Abd al-Barr in *al-Istī'āb*, vol. 2, p. 163.

Then the Holy Prophet (blessings and peace be upon him) asked his enemies: “What kind of behaviour do you expect from me today?” They replied: “We expect the same behaviour as the one Prophet Yūsuf extended to his brothers.” The Holy Prophet (blessings and peace be upon him) said what Prophet Yūsuf had announced:

«اذْهَبُوا فَأَنْتُمُ الطُّلَقَاءُ».

“Go, for you are free (of all blame and punishment).”[41]

This is one of the many examples illustrating the magnanimity of the Prophet Muḥammad (blessings and peace be upon him). At that time one of his greatest opponents were Abū Sufyān and his two sons. However, after the conquest of Makkah, the Prophet Muḥammad (blessings and peace be upon him) declared the house of Abū Sufyān secure such that whosoever entered it would be protected.[42] The sons of Abū Lahab, a vehement enemy of Islām, feared being killed so they hid under the covering of the *ka'ba* but when the Holy Prophet (blessings and peace be upon him) found them he forgave them.[43] Through such gracious conduct the Prophet Muḥammad (blessings and peace be upon him) single-handedly united Arabia and left behind for his followers a legacy of love, compassion and tolerance.

Those who claim that Islām was spread by the sword and that it advocates perpetual warfare, need only to sincerely study the life of the Prophet (blessings and peace be upon him) and early Islāmic history. One will undoubtedly find that the Prophet (blessings and peace be upon him) never initiated a war against the Makkans. In

---

41 Related by Ibn Ḥajar al-'Asqalānī in *Fatḥ al-Bārī*, vol. 8, pp. 18, 19.

42 Related by Muslim in *al-Ṣaḥīḥ*, vol. 3, pp. 1405-1408 # 1780; Abū Dāwūd in *al-Sunan*, vol. 3, p. 197 # 3021; and al-Dāraquṭnī in *al-Sunan*, vol. 3, p. 60 # 233.

43 Related by Zayla'ī in *Naṣb al-Rāya*, vol. 3, p. 336.

fact, both the battles of Badr and Uḥud were fought on the borders of Medina and the Prophet (blessings and peace be upon him) was defending his City. Aggression and violence were not part of his noble nature and his life and teachings are a testimony to that. Human history has never witnessed an individual as wholly and utterly devoted to the principles of peace like the Prophet (blessings and peace be upon him).

9.4 ISLAMIC LAW PRESCRIBES JUSTICE AND EQUITY FOR NON-MUSLIMS

Books of Prophetic traditions are replete with noble sayings, which expound the loftiest ethical principles humankind ever knew. The Prophet (blessings and peace be upon him) was a fount of justice, love and mercy. His character epitomised human dignity. He (blessings and peace be upon him) said,

«أَنَا أَحَقُّ مَنْ وَفَى بِذِمَّتِهِ».

"I am the most worthy of those who fulfill their responsibility (I.e. with regards non-Muslims)."[44]

'Alī b. Abī Ṭālib (may Allāh be well pleased with him) said:

«إِذَا قَتَلَ الْمُسْلِمُ النَّصْرَانِيَّ قُتِلَ بِهِ».

"If a Muslim kills a Christian, he will be killed (in retaliation)."[45]

---

44 Set forth by al-Shāfi'ī in *al-Musnad*, pp. 343, 344 and *al-Umm*, vol. 7, p. 320; Abū Nu'aym in *Musnad Abī Ḥanīfa*, p. 104; al-Shaybānī in *al-Mabsūṭ*, vol. 4, p. 488; al-Bayhaqī in *al-Sunan al-Kubrā*, vol. 8, p. 30 # 15696.

45 Related by al-Shaybānī in *al-Ḥujja*, vol. 4, p. 349; al-Shāfi'ī in *al-Umm*, vol. 7, p. 320; and al-Shawkānī in *Nayl al-Awṭār*, vol. 7, p. 154.

9.5 THE BLOOD MONEY (DIYYA) OF A NON-MUSLIM IS EQUAL TO THAT OF A MUSLIM

Imam Abū Ḥanīfa said:

دِيَّةُ الْيَهُوْدِيِّ وَالنَّصْرَانِيِّ وَالْمَجُوْسِيِّ مِثْلُ دِيَّةِ الْحُرِّ الْمُسْلِمِ.

"The Blood-money of a Jew, Christian and Magnus is equal to that of a free Muslim."[46]

'Amr b. al-'Āṣ (may Allāh be well pleased with him) was the Governor of Egypt and his son gave an illegal punishment to a non-Muslim. The case was referred to 'Umar (may Allāh be well pleased with him), who gave punishment to the son of 'Amr b. al-'Āṣ (may Allāh be well pleased with him) openly and said to him:

مُذْ كَمْ اسْتَعْبَدْتُمُ النَّاسَ وَقَدْ وَلَدَتْهُمْ أُمَّهَاتُهُمْ أَحْرَارًا؟

"Since when have you made people your slaves when their mother gave birth to them as free men?"[47]

Renowned *ḥadīth*-scholar Ibn Shahāb al-Zuhrī states that during the caliphate of Abū Bakr, 'Umar and 'Uthmān (may Allāh be well pleased with them) the blood money of the non-Muslims citizens of the Islāmic state was equal to that of Muslims.[48]

It is mentioned by Ibn Sa'd in *al-Ṭabaqāt al-Kubrā* (vol. 1, p. 358) that the Holy Prophet (blessings and peace be upon him) wrote a

---

46 Related by Ibn Abī Shayba in al-Muṣannaf, vol. 5, p. 407 # 27448; 'Abd al-Razzāq in al-Muṣannaf, vol. 10, pp. 95, 97, 99; al-Shaybānī in *al-Ḥujja*, vol. 4, pp. 322, 323; and al-Shawkānī in *Nayl al-Awṭār*, vol. 7, p. 154.

47 Related by al-Hindī in *Kanz al-'Ummāl*, vol. 12, pp. 660, 661 # 36010.

48 Related by al-Shaybānī in *al-Ḥujja*, vol. 4, p. 351; and al-Shawkānī in *Nayl al-Awṭār*, vol. 7, p. 321.

letter to the people of Najrān when they had announced their affiliation to the Islāmic state of Medina. That letter says:

«لِنَجْرَانَ وَحَاشِيَتِهِمْ جِوَارُ اللهِ وَذِمَّةُ مُحَمَّدٍ النَّبِيِّ رَسُوْلِ اللهِ ﷺ عَلَى أَنْفُسِهِمْ وَمِلَّتِهِمْ وَأَرْضِهِمْ وَأَمْوَالِهِمْ وَغَائِبِهِمْ وَشَاهِدِهِمْ وَبِيَعِهِمْ، لَا يُغَيِّرُوا أُسْقُفْ عَنْ سَقِيْفَاهُ، وَلَا رَاهِبٌ عَنْ رَهْبَانِيَّتِهِ، وَلَا وَاقِفٌ عَنْ وَقْفَانِيَّتِهِ».

"Najrān and its allies (who have accepted the authority of the State of Medina) have the guaranteed protection of Allāh and the Prophet Muḥammad, Allāh's Messenger; (this protection extends) to their lives, religion, land, wealth; to all those who are present or absent as well as their business. (It is also my order for the Muslim government that) no priest, monk or chief is removed from his office."

9.6 SOCIAL BENEFITS AND INCOME SUPPORT FOR JOBLESS, OLD, OR DISABLED NON-MUSLIMS LIVING IN AN ISLAMIC STATE

The Prophet (blessings and peace be upon him) and the orthodox Caliphs declared that the non-Muslims in the Islāmic state would be entitled to all social benefits that the Muslims were entitled to. Assistance was provided for elderly and ill non-Muslims as it was provided for the Muslims. It is reported by Sa'īd b. al-Musayyab that the Prophet (blessings and peace be upon him) gave charity to a Jewish house and it was being practised after the demise of the Holy Prophet (blessings and peace be upon him).[49]

---

49 Abū 'Ubayd al-Qāsim b. Sallām, *Kitāb al-Amwāl*, p. 543 # 1992.

'Amr b. Maymūn, 'Amr b. Sharjīl and Murra Hamdhānī stated that they used to give a portion of charity of *fiṭr* to Christian monks.[50]

Al-Imām Yūsuf stated: "If non-Muslim citizens of the Islāmic state became jobless, old, or disabled then they would be legally entitled to social benefit and income support."[51]

This model of conduct was also adopted by the Caliphs of the Prophet (blessings and peace be upon him). For instance, 'Umar b. al-Khaṭṭāb (may Allāh be well pleased with him) saw an old Jewish citizen of Medina begging and he asked him: *"Why are you begging?" The Jew replied: "I have to pay the tax that's why I am begging and I am jobless."* 'Umar (may Allāh be well pleased with him) helped him *financially.* He then sent him to the secretary of finance and said: *"From today all Jews, Christians and non-Muslims who are jobless or who are old and unable to earn are exempted from the national taxes for their security and they are entitled to income support and social benefit."*[52]

9.7 JEWS AND CHRISTIANS ENJOYED A MULTI-CULTURAL COEXISTENCE IN MUSLIM LANDS

Throughout Islāmic history both Jews and Christians enjoyed hostile-free existence in Muslim lands. In cases where injustices have been committed against the non-Muslims by the Muslims, orders have been passed against the latter to correct their wrongs. Balādharī says in *Futūḥ al-Buldān* (p. 150), that during 'Umar b. 'Abd al-'Azīz's caliphate a part of a church was demolished and included into a mosque. The case was referred to the Caliph who ordered that the part of the mosque should be demolished and the land returned to the Christians so that they could re-build their church.

These are a handful of examples to illustrate the position accorded to non-Muslims in an Islāmic state. Islām teaches respect

---

50 Abū 'Ubayd al-Qāsim b. Sallām, *Kitāb al-Amwāl*, p. 543 # 1997.

51 Abū Yūsuf, *Kitāb al-Kharāj*, pp. 122, 125.

52 Ibn Qudāma, *al-Mughnī*, vol. 8, pp. 507-511; Abū Yūsuf, *Kitāb al-Kharāj*, p. 125.

for other religions and it holds itself responsible for the protection of churches and other places of worship. In the Islāmic state Christians were permitted to sing Christmas songs during Christmas except for at the time of the five obligatory prayers. Islāmic rule commanded that their religion, culture and practice should never be interfered with and that they should enjoy complete religious freedom.

Moreover there were written instructions from the Holy Prophet (blessings and peace be upon him) and the Caliphs that non-Muslims would never be forced to perform state defence duties, but their protection was the responsibility of the state.[53] Military commanders were given a commandment by Abū Bakr (may Allāh be well pleased with him) which has been reported by al-Bayhaqī, that during wartime the captured lands of non-Muslims should come to no harm. The trees should not be cut, their cattle should not be killed and their places of worship should not be demolished. If religious leaders were confined in the act of worship in their churches they should not be disturbed as they are not combatants. No harm should be caused to even the general population in their homes.[54]

In light of the primary evidences and its substantiations presented above it is manifest that those 'Muslims' who adhere to ideologies of violence and indiscriminate killings, and those who condone suicide bombings, all in the name of Islām, are most certainly not adherents of the Prophetic paradigm.

---

53 Kāsānī, *Badā'i' al-Ṣanā'i'*, vol. 7, pp. 112, 113; al-Shurbīnī, *Mughnī al-Muḥtāj*, vol. 4, p. 243.

54 Related by al-Bayhaqī in *al-Sunan al-Kubrā*, vol. 9, p. 85 # 17904.

10. THE TREATY OF HUDAYBIYYA: A SHINING SYMBOL OF THE PROPHETIC PREFERENCE FOR PEACE OVER CONFLICT

An interesting case study of the Prophet's conduct in times of tension and turbulence, is the occasion of the *Treaty of Ḥudaybiyya*. In the year 628, the Prophet Muḥammad (blessings and peace be upon him) set out to perform the pilgrimage, with about 1400 unarmed companions, dressed in two pieces of unsown cloth, known as the Ihram. Upon hearing of the Prophet's intentions, the Makkan leaders and neighbouring tribes took up arms and were determined to deter the Muslims from entering the Holy vicinity. The Makkan armies, together with their allies, marched out of Makka and awaited the Prophet's arrival. When the Muslims arrived at Ḥudaybiyya, a place several miles from Makka, the Prophet (blessings and peace be upon him) ordered the Muslims to camp, and then selected 'Uthman b. 'Affan (may Allāh be please with him) as his emissary, to go and negotiate with the Makkan leaders, which ultimately proved unsuccessful. Finally, the Makkans sent a delegation headed by Suhayl b. 'Amr, and the negotiations resulted in the treaty of Ḥudaybiyya.

Under the terms of the treaty, the Prophet Muḥammad (blessings and peace be upon him) would be allowed to make the pilgrimage the following year and was thus denied entry into Makkah. The holy vicinity would be emptied for three days for the Muslim pilgrims. The treaty also stipulated a truce for ten years. Any tribe or person would be free to join either party or make an alliance with it; the slaves amongst the Makkans, who had left paganism and accepted Islām were to be returned to the Makkans by the Muslims.

This last condition was not reciprocal and was objected to in the Muslim camp. Senior Companions such as 'Umar b. al-Khaṭṭāb (may Allāh be well pleased with him) were shocked that the Prophet (blessings and peace be upon him) could accept such a biased stipulation. The Prophet Muḥammad (blessings and peace be upon him) responded to all objections with wisdom and told his followers that they would understand the reasons behind his decisions. As the treaty was signed, Abū Jandal, the son of Suhayl, the head of the Makkan delegation, came, trailing his chains, in order to join the Muslims. God's Messenger (blessings and peace be upon him) had to return him to his father in tears, in order to abide by the conditions of the treaty. This again upset the Prophet's (blessings and peace be upon him) followers and again he taught them to be patient and await success from God.

Prophet Muḥammad (blessings and peace be upon him) asked 'Alī (may Allāh be well pleased with him) to write down the treaty and Suhayl b. 'Amr a representative of the Makkans witnessed it. Upon noticing that the treaty began in the Name of God, Suhayl objected and asserted that it be removed. The Prophet Muḥammad (blessings and peace be upon him) instructed 'Alī to remove it. Suhayl again objected when 'Alī (may Allāh be pleased with him) wrote the name of the Prophet Muḥammad with the appellation 'the Messenger of God'. The Prophet (blessings and peace be upon him) instructed 'Ali to remove it, but he could not bring himself to do so. The Prophet (blessings and peace be upon him) then took it upon himself to comply with the demand of the Makkans. By doing thus, neither was his Prophecy negated nor did it lower his status in the eyes of those around him. In fact, his conduct amplified his nobility further and as with all his noble acts, this was also a harbinger of peace.

Another condition of the treaty, which was not favourable to the Muslims, was to return to Medina without having performed the pilgrimage. The Prophet (blessings and peace be upon him) instructed his followers to remove their iḥrām and sacrifice their animals but none of the followers complied. They were in a state of shock and distressed at having reached their destination only to turn away without having fulfilled their purpose. Thrice Prophet Muḥammad (blessings and peace be upon him) instructed them and all three times they refused to obey. Upon the advice of his wife Umm Salama (may Allāh be well pleased with her) the Prophet (blessings and peace be upon him) removed his iḥrām and slaughtered his camel. Upon seeing this, the Companions removed their iḥrām and sacrificed an animal.[55]

These strategic actions undertaken by Prophet Muḥammad (blessings and peace be upon him) only reinforced the belief his followers had in his message and enhanced the security of his people. Complying with the Makkans, to engender peace and security, was his main objective and by acquiescing to their demands this lofty objective was achieved.

55 Related by al-Bukhārī in *al-Saḥīḥ*, vol. 2, pp. 974-979 # 2580.

11. THE WEST AND MUSLIM MINORITIES

11.1 UNDERSTANDING AND TACKLING EXTREMISM AND TERRORISM

If the West truly wishes to eliminate terrorism they must begin by identifying their enemies. These terrorists are no more than a handful of misguided people whose religious life is based either on misinterpretation or ignorance of the religious teachings. It is also important that they do not confine extremism to Islām, or any other religion for that matter, for it is found amongst followers of all religious traditions. Extremism has no religion and it most certainly has no place in Islām. Rather, terrorism is an attitude and a social behaviour, which arises from frustration and nihilism. Terrorist activity may also reflect the vested interests of the agencies that wish to attain certain aims and objectives.

The incessant attempts to connect Islām and terrorism, as though they are absolutely inseparable, has led to the infusion of antagonism in the hearts and minds of young Muslims; hence the widespread expressions of hatred and animosity. The West must also discontinue its support for Muslim countries with extremist attitudes. I personally know of many countries that not only financially support extremists and their projects but also provide them with political protection. The causes of terrorism are multifarious and it is the underlying causes that must be tackled; be they political, psychological or sociological.

11.2 MUSLIMS: INTEGRATION, ISOLATION, OR ANNIHILATION

The Medinian society, established by the Prophet Muḥammad (blessings and peace be upon him) himself, was built on the principle of integration and was as such a categorical rejection of the models of isolation and annihilation, the former of which would have left his community cut off from the rest of the world and the latter, devoid of a definite identity, unique to them.

Muslims living in Britain, America and Europe have a choice. They either follow the path the Prophet Muḥammad (blessings and peace be upon him) took and integrate into the British society by abiding by the law of the land, participating in the political process, and at the same time fulfil their obligations as Muslims. In contradistinction, they may go against the Prophet's teachings and instead, live in ghettoised areas, hostile to other communities and unwilling to participate in any form of communal structure. Views and propagations that suggest such ideologies are to be shunned and abandoned in their entirety.

11.3 CLOSING: THE PROPHETS FINAL SERMON - A FORERUNNER TO THE UNIVERSAL DECLARATION OF HUMAN RIGHTS

In his Farewell sermon, the Prophet Muḥammad (blessings and peace be upon him) addressed a gathering of more than a hundred thousand people, summarising his teachings for them, as well as reminding them of his life-long struggle in upholding the highest moral principles that humankind ever witnessed. In this historic sermon, he spoke of racial equality, tolerance and peace. In fact the basis for a declaration of human rights was established through this sermon alone. Superiority of one human being over any other was quashed, except by individual excellence and conscientiousness. Thus excellence of moral character was to be the only criterion of individual superiority in the eyes of God. The rights of each and every human being pertaining to their person, property and honour were declared sacrosanct.

At the domestic front, his sermon banished oppression and centuries of subjugation of women by declaring them as equals to men.

Before his arrival, Arabia was fraught with deceit and corruption in trade and commerce, so he eliminated economic exploitation by enforcing just trade, as well as the right to ownership and inheritance. He declared fulfilling the rights of the state an obligation upon all Muslims, thus ensuring that they live as peaceful citizens wherever they may be. His message was not only for the thousands standing before him but for Muslims of all places and times. It was a universal message, whose teachings resonate in the corners of the earth, such that the Universal Declaration of Human Rights is based on the same concepts.

This is a brief exposition of the magnanimous conduct of the Prophet of Islām. The reality is that no amount of words can truly capture the grandeur of that Man whose noble teachings gave rise to an empire of peace and mercy. The Qur'ān and the Prophetic Sunna are his legacy and will last forever, thus ensuring that every age will see for itself the miracles of his conduct.

- PART 2 -
RENOUNCING TERROR, REGAINING PEACE, AND THE FUTURE OF ISLAM

1. AUTHORS PREFACE

THIS LECTURE WILL put the three parts of the title together into a single coherent narrative with the aim of imbuing greater clarity and lucidity than if they were addressed separately. There is no doubt that we are living in a crucial and critical time, with the Muslim community as a whole, and the younger generation in particular, facing a terrible situation in connection to their Islāmic faith, particularly in the West. A monstrous image of the faith has been painted by the media, creating misunderstanding and confusion amongst both Muslims and non-Muslims. Likewise, those who are engaged in the propagation of Islām and its defence, act in a way that does not serve the Islāmic objectives but rather plays into the hands of their antagonists. Instead of imitating this approach, in order to understand this case in the light of the basic teachings and prescriptions of Islām it would be better to refer the whole case to the Qur'ān, Sunna and the sīra of the Holy Prophet Muḥammad (blessings and peace be upon him). Thus this discourse will be clarifying the true essence of Islām commencing with its lexical meaning, thereafter going onto its true nature and basic teachings with the intention of determining where this noble religion stands in connection to peace and terrorism.

2. LEXICAL AND TECHNICAL MEANINGS OF ISLĀM, ĪMĀN, AND IḤSĀN

There are three basic postulations that underpin Islāmic thought: Islām, Īmān, and Iḥsān. Islām is the practical dimension of the religion which deals with the outward; Īmān is its theological dimension which deals with thoughts and beliefs; and Iḥsān is the spiritual dimension, concerned with achieving internal excellence and perfection. As for the lexical implications of these words it is interesting to note that the word Islām is derived from the root word silm, which denotes peace, discipline and obedience,[56] whilst the word īmān is derived from the root word aman and amn which signifies peace, safety and security.[57] Iḥsān is derived from husn which means excellence and beauty.[58] Before we proceed in elaborating this concept it is necessary to repel a misgiving when discussing the significance of peace in the Islāmic teachings and when rejecting terrorism. There are primarily two kinds of reactions to this discussion: the first is of the sceptics who do not understand the real teachings of the religion, holding the misguided viewpoint that any discussion on the concept of peace in Islām as nothing but a mere strategy aiming to give a peaceful face to the tradition; the second is of a number of Muslims themselves who, when hearing talk of peace, assume that Muslims have become apologetic in the face of western aggression and that there is no need to become defensive. To clarify, this essay is neither a defence strategy nor is it apologetic: it is an attempt to relay the real message of Islām.

---

56 Ibn Manẓūr, *Lisān al-'Arab*, vol. 12, p. 289.

57 Ibn Manẓūr, *Lisān al-'Arab*, vol. 13, p. 21.

58 Abū Manṣūr al-Azharī, *Tahdhīb al-Lugha*, vol. 4, p. 182; Ibn Manẓūr, *Lisān al-'Arab*, vol. 13, p. 114.

To begin with *Islām*, Almighty Allāh and the Prophet Muḥammad (blessings and peace be upon him) have declared that the best of Islām is to propagate and practice peace, having stated:

«تُطْعِمُ الطَّعَامَ وَتَقْرَأُ السَّلَامَ عَلَى مَنْ عَرَفْتَ وَمَنْ لَمْ تَعْرِفْ».

"(The best action in Islām is that) you serve the food, and recite the salutation of peace to someone whether you know him or do not know!" [59]

In emulation of this noble precinct set by the Prophet Muḥammad (blessings and peace be upon him), Muslims greet with the formula of peace: al-sālam-u 'alaykum meaning 'peace be unto you', and conclude prayers by uttering the words of peace when turning one's head to the right and the left: al-sālam-u 'alaykum wa raḥmat'ul-llāh which translates to 'peace be upon you and mercy of Allāh.' This is a proclamation of peace to those sat on either side. Similarly, when the believers enter the gates of Paradise they will be greeted with the words of peace as recorded in the Qur'ān: Almighty Allāh and the angels will receive them saying

﴿تَحِيَّتُهُمْ يَوْمَ يَلْقَوْنَهُۥ سَلَٰمٌ﴾.

'On the Day when they (the believers) will meet Him, their gift (of the meeting — greeting) will be: 'Peace!" [60]

The epithet of Paradise, as given by Almighty Allāh, is *Dār al-Salām*, or 'the abode of peace'. Among the many names and attributes of

---

[59] Related by al-Bukhārī in *al-Ṣaḥīḥ*, vol. 1, pp. 13, 19 # 12, 28; and Muslim in *al-Ṣaḥīḥ*, vol. 1, p. 65 # 39.

[60] Al-Qur'ān, *al-Aḥzāb*, 33: 44.

God, one of the most significant is the name *al-Salām*: God is peace. After each prayer in conformity to the noble practice of the Prophet Muḥammad (blessings and peace be upon him), the Muslims plead unto God, invoking Him with the following supplication:

«اللَّهُمَّ أَنْتَ السَّلَامُ وَمِنْكَ السَّلَامُ، تَبَارَكْتَ يا ذَا الْجَلَالِ وَالْإِكْرَامِ».

"O Allah: You are Peace, and peace comes from You, blessed are You, Possessor of Glory and Honour."[61]

In another narration related by Makḥūl and transmitted by al-Bayhaqī, it is stated when the Holy Prophet (blessings and peace be upon him) entered Makka and saw the House of Allah, he raised his hands, glorified the greatness and majesty of Almighty Allah and prayed with these words:

«اللَّهُمَّ أَنْتَ السَّلَامُ وَمِنْكَ السَّلَامُ، فَحَيِّنَا رَبَّنَا بِالسَّلَامِ».

"O Allah: You are Peace, and peace comes from You. O our Lord! Give us a life of peace."[62]

The three words *Islām*, *Īmān*, and *Iḥsān* originate from the famous Tradition of Gabriel, in which he came to the Prophet (blessings and peace be upon him) in the guise of a Bedouin to teach the

---

61 Related by Muslim in *al-Ṣaḥīḥ*, vol. 1, p. 414 # 591, 592; Abū Dāwūd in *al-Sunan*, vol. 1, p. 474 # 1512; al-Tirmidhī in *al-Sunan*, vol. 2, p. 95, # 298; al-Nasā'ī in *al-Sunan*, vol. 3, pp. 68, 69 # 1337, 1338; Ibn Māja in *al-Sunan*, vol. 1, pp. 298, 300 # 924, 928.

62 Related by al-Bayhaqī in *al-Sunan al-Kubrā*, vol. 5, p. 73 # 8995.

Companions (may Allāh be well pleased with them) their religion. The tradition related by 'Umar b. al-Khaṭṭāb (may Allāh be well pleased with him) is as follows:

بَيْنَمَا نَحْنُ عِنْدَ رَسُوْلِ اللهِ ﷺ ذَاتَ يَوْمٍ إِذْ طَلَعَ عَلَيْنَا رَجُلٌ شَدِيْدُ بَيَاضِ الثِّيَابِ، شَدِيْدُ سَوَادِ الشَّعْرِ. لاَ يُرَى عَلَيْهِ أَثَرُ السَّفَرِ، وَلاَ يَعْرِفُهُ مِنَّا أَحَدٌ، حَتَّى جَلَسَ إِلَى النَّبِيِّ ﷺ، فَأَسْنَدَ رُكْبَتَيْهِ إِلَى رُكْبَتَيْهِ، وَوَضَعَ كَفَّيْهِ عَلَى فَخِذَيْهِ، وَقَالَ: يَا مُحَمَّدُ! أَخْبِرْنِي عَنِ الإِسْلاَمِ. فَقَالَ رَسُوْلُ اللهِ ﷺ: «الإِسْلاَمُ أَنْ تَشْهَدَ أَنْ لاَ إِلَهَ إِلاَّ اللهُ، وَأَنَّ مُحَمَّدًا رَسُوْلُ اللهِ، وَتُقِيمَ الصَّلاَةَ، وَتُؤْتِيَ الزَّكَاةَ، وَتَصُوْمَ رَمَضَانَ، وَتَحُجَّ الْبَيْتَ إِنِ اسْتَطَعْتَ إِلَيْهِ سَبِيْلاً». قَالَ: صَدَقْتَ. قَالَ: فَعَجِبْنَا لَهُ يَسْأَلُهُ وَيُصَدِّقُهُ! قَالَ: فَأَخْبِرْنِي عَنِ الإِيْمَانِ. قَالَ: «أَنْ تُؤْمِنَ بِاللهِ، وَمَلاَئِكَتِهِ، وَكُتُبِهِ، وَرُسُلِهِ، وَالْيَوْمِ الآخِرِ،

وَتُؤْمِنَ بِالْقَدَرِ خَيْرِهِ وَشَرِّهِ». قَالَ: صَدَقْتَ.
قَالَ: فَأَخْبِرْنِي عَنِ الإِحْسَانِ. قَالَ: «أَنْ تَعْبُدَ
اللهَ كَأَنَّكَ تَرَاهُ، فَإِنْ لَمْ تَكُنْ تَرَاهُ فَإِنَّهُ يَرَاكَ».
... ثُمَّ انْطَلَقَ، فَلَبِثْتُ مَلِيّاً، ثُمَّ قَالَ: يَا عُمَرُ!
«أَتَدْرِي مَنِ السَّائِلُ»؟ قُلْتُ: اللهُ وَرَسُولُهُ
أَعْلَمُ. قَالَ: «فَإِنَّهُ جِبْرِيلُ، أَتَاكُمْ يُعَلِّمُكُمْ
دِينَكُمْ».

'As we sat one day with the Messenger of Allāh (blessings and peace be upon him), a man in pure white clothing and jet black hair came to us, without a trace of travelling upon him, though none of us knew him. He sat down before the Prophet (blessings and peace be upon him) bracing his knees against his, resting his hands on his legs, and said: " O Muḥammad, tell me about Islām." The Messenger of Allāh (blessings and peace be upon him) said: "Islām is to testify that there is no God but Allāh and that Muḥammad is the Messenger of Allāh, and to perform the prayer, give zakāt, fast in Ramaḍān, and perform the pilgrimage to the House if you can find a way." He said: "You have spoken the truth," and we were surprised that he should ask and then confirm the answer. Then he said: "Tell me about true faith (Īmān)" and the Prophet (blessings and peace be upon him) answered: "It is to believe in Allāh, His angels, His inspired Books, His messengers, the Last Day, and in destiny, it's good and evil." "You have spoken the truth," he said, "Now tell me about the perfection of faith (Iḥsān)," and the Prophet (blessings and peace be upon him) answered: "It is to worship Allāh as if you see Him, and if you see Him not, He nevertheless sees you." ... Then the visitor left. I waited a long while, and the Prophet (blessings and peace be upon him) said to me, "Do you know, 'Umar, who was the questioner?" and I replied, "Allāh and His

Messenger know best." He said, "It was Gabriel, who came to you to teach you your religion.'"[63]

These three terms (which are three grades of the religion of Islām as well) were also spoken by God in the Qur'ān, and it is interesting to note that Almighty Allāh has chosen specific words to prescribe and illustrate the concept of *Islām*, *Īmān* and *Iḥsān*.

Concerning *Islām*, the first grade of Islām, God says in the Qur'ān:

﴿ٱلْيَوْمَ أَكْمَلْتُ لَكُمْ دِينَكُمْ وَأَتْمَمْتُ عَلَيْكُمْ نِعْمَتِى وَرَضِيتُ لَكُمُ ٱلْإِسْلَـٰمَ دِينًا ۚ﴾.

"Today I have perfected for you your religion and I have completed the bestowal of My mercy upon you, and I am pleased to choose Islām as your religion."[64]

Here the word *raḍītu* (derived from *riḍā*; pleasure) is linked with the word Islām. Likewise concerning the second grade of Islām, *Īmān*, the Qur'ān states:

﴿قَالَتِ ٱلْأَعْرَابُ ءَامَنَّا ۖ قُل لَّمْ تُؤْمِنُوا۟ وَلَـٰكِن قُولُوٓا۟ أَسْلَمْنَا وَلَمَّا يَدْخُلِ ٱلْإِيمَـٰنُ فِى قُلُوبِكُمْ ۖ﴾.

---

63 Related by al-Bukhārī in *al-Ṣaḥīḥ*, vol. 1, p. 27 # 50; vol. 4, p. 1793 # 4499; Muslim in *al-Ṣaḥīḥ*, vol. 1, p. 36 # 8, 9; al-Tirmidhī in *al-Sunan*, vol. 5, p. 6 # 2610, Abū Dāwūd in *al-Sunan*, vol. 4, p. 359 # 4697; al-Nasā'ī in *al-Sunan*, vol. 8, p. 97 # 4990; Ibn Māja in *al-Sunan*, vol. 1, p. 24 # 63; Aḥmad b. Ḥanbal in *al-Musnad*, vol. 1, p. 51 # 367; Ibn Khuzayma in *al-Ṣaḥīḥ*, vol. 4, p. 127 # 2504; and Ibn Ḥibbān in *al-Ṣaḥīḥ*, vol. 1, p. 389 # 168.

64 Al-Qur'ān, *al-Mā'ida*, 5: 3.

"The Bedouins say: 'We have believed.' Say: 'You have not believed. Yes, rather say: We have accepted Islam. And the belief has not yet gone into your hearts.'" [65]

At another place, the Qur'ān states about the second grade of Islām in these words:

﴿وَلَٰكِنَّ ٱللَّهَ حَبَّبَ إِلَيۡكُمُ ٱلۡإِيمَٰنَ وَزَيَّنَهُۥ فِي قُلُوبِكُمۡ﴾.

"But Allāh has blessed you with the love of faith and has embellished it in your hearts." [66]

In this verse, Almighty Allāh has chosen two words to explain *Īmān*; one is *maḥabba* (love) and the other is *zīna* (beauty).

Finally, *Iḥsān*, which is the third and excellent grade of the religion of Islām, is imbued with the concept of eliminating mischief and corruption from the world. Almighty Allāh states:

﴿وَأَحۡسِن كَمَآ أَحۡسَنَ ٱللَّهُ إِلَيۡكَۖ وَلَا تَبۡغِ ٱلۡفَسَادَ فِي ٱلۡأَرۡضِۖ﴾.

"And do (such) good (to the people) as Allāh has done good to you. But do not look for (ways to spread) evil and terror in the land (through oppression, accumulation of wealth and exploitation)." [67]

In this verse *Iḥsān* has been connected with negation of *fasād*, i.e. this verse instructs the believer to adopt the practice of *Iḥsān* and

---

65 Al-Qur'ān, *al-Ḥujurāt*, 49: 14.

66 Al-Qur'ān, *al-Ḥujurāt*, 49: 7.

67 Al-Qur'ān, *al-Qaṣaṣ*, 28: 77.

thus eliminate corruption from the world. The choice of words used to illustrate the concepts of *Islām, Īmān and Iḥsān* therefore pose a significant relevance.

Also noteworthy are the definitions of a Muslim and a mu'min, meaning a true believer, as explained by the Prophet Muḥammad (blessings and peace be upon him).

According to 'Abd Allāh b. 'Amr b. al-'Āṣ (may Allāh be well pleased with him), Allāh's Messenger (blessings and peace be upon him) said:

«اَلْمُسْلِمُ مَنْ سَلِمَ الْمُسْلِمُوْنَ مِنْ لِسَانِهِ وَيَدِهِ».

"A Muslim is the one who provides peace to other Muslims through his words and deeds." [68]

A *mu'min* was described as:

«اَلْمُؤْمِنُ مَنْ أَمِنَهُ النَّاسُ عَلَى دِمَائِهِمْ

وَأَمْوَالِهِمْ».

"The mu'min is someone whom people trust with regard to their blood and their properties." [69]

Thus, a true believer is the one who provides peace and security for not only Muslims but non-Muslims alike.

In another tradition transmitted by Shaddād b. Aws (may Allāh be well pleased with him), the Prophet (blessings and peace be upon him) said of *Iḥsān*:

---

[68] Related by al-Bukhārī in *al-Ṣaḥīḥ*, vol. 1, p. 13 # 10; Muslim in *al-Ṣaḥīḥ*, vol. 1, p. 65 # 41; al-Tirmidhī in *al-Sunan*, vol. 5, p. 17 # 2627; Aḥmad b. Ḥanbal in *al-Musnad*, vol. 3, p. 440 # 15673; and Ibn Ḥibbān in *al-Ṣaḥīḥ*, vol. 1, p. 406 # 180.

[69] Related by al-Nasā'ī in *al-Sunan*, vol. 8, p. 104 # 4995; and Aḥmad b. Ḥanbal in *al-Musnad*, vol. 2, p. 379 # 8918.

«إِنَّ اللهَ كَتَبَ الإِحْسَانَ عَلَى كُلِّ شَيءٍ، فَإِذَا قَتَلْتُمْ فَأَحْسِنُوا الْقِتْلَةَ، وَإِذَا ذَبَحْتُمْ فَأَحْسِنُوا الذَّبْحَ، وَلْيُحِدَّ أَحَدُكُمْ شَفْرَتَهُ، فَلْيُرِحْ ذَبِيحَتَهُ».

"Allāh has prescribed spiritual excellence in the treatment of everything, so if you kill (any combatant during war), you must perform the killing with moral excellence (causing the least torture), and if you sacrifice an animal, you must perform the slaughter most caringly, and let one of you sharpen his blade, in order to set his sacrificial animal at rest (causing it least discomfort)!" [70]

In a state of war disposition for benevolence is commanded and at the same time infliction of terror is sternly prohibited. In the same cruelty to animals is also forbidden even during slaughter.

Furthermore, the Prophet (blessings and peace be upon him) said:

«اَلْخَلْقُ كُلُّهُمْ عِيَالُ اللهِ، فَأَحَبُّ الْخَلْقِ إِلَى اللهِ أَنْفَعُهُمْ لِعِيَالِهِ».

"The whole of creation is the dependent (family) of Allāh. So the dearest one to Him, from amongst them, is the one most beneficial to His family." [71]

70 Related by Muslim in *al-Ṣaḥīḥ*, vol. 3, p. 1548 # 1955; al-Tirmidhī in *al-Sunan*, vol. 4, p. 23 # 1409; Abū Dāwūd in *al-Sunan*, vol. 3, p. 58 # 2817; al-Nasā'ī in *al-Sunan*, vol. 7, p. 227 # 4405; and Ibn Māja in *al-Sunan*, vol. 2, p. 1058 # 3170.

71 Related by al-Ṭabarānī in *al-Mu'jam al-Kabīr*, vol. 10, p. 86 # 10033, and *al-Mu'jam al-Awsaṭ*, vol. 5, p. 356 # 5541; Abū Ya'lā in *al-Musnad*, vol. 6, pp. 65, 106, 194 # 3315, 3370, 3478; al-Shāshī in *al-Musnad*, vol. 1, p. 419 # 435; and al-Qaḍā'ī in *Musnad al-Shihāb*, vol. 2, p. 255 # 1306.

3. THE CONCEPT OF BALANCE IN ISLAM

The aforementioned traditions are a brief exposition of the concepts and implications of *Islām*, *Īmān*, and *Iḥsān*. What follows now is a brief discourse on the concepts of balance, tolerance and moderation in light of the Qur'ān and Prophetic tradition.

The Holy Qur'ān explains that,

﴿وَلَقَدۡ خَلَقۡنَا ٱلۡإِنسَٰنَ مِن سُلَٰلَةٖ مِّن طِينٖ ١٢
ثُمَّ جَعَلۡنَٰهُ نُطۡفَةٗ فِي قَرَارٖ مَّكِينٖ ١٣ ثُمَّ خَلَقۡنَا
ٱلنُّطۡفَةَ عَلَقَةٗ فَخَلَقۡنَا ٱلۡعَلَقَةَ مُضۡغَةٗ فَخَلَقۡنَا
ٱلۡمُضۡغَةَ عِظَٰمٗا فَكَسَوۡنَا ٱلۡعِظَٰمَ لَحۡمٗا ثُمَّ
أَنشَأۡنَٰهُ خَلۡقًا ءَاخَرَۚ فَتَبَارَكَ ٱللَّهُ أَحۡسَنُ
ٱلۡخَٰلِقِينَ ١٤﴾

"And indeed We originated (the genesis of) man from the extract of (chemical ingredients of) clay. Then We placed him as a sperm drop (zygote) in a secure place (mother's womb). Then We made that zygote a hanging mass (clinging to the uterus like a leech). Then We developed that hanging mass into a lump, looking chewed with teeth. Out of this chewed lump We built a structure of bones which We clothed with flesh (and muscles). Then (changing him) into another form We developed him (gradually) into a new creation. Then Allāh brought (him up into a strong body), Allāh — the Best of creators."[72]

---

[72] Al-Qur'ān, *al-Mu'minūn*, 23: 12-14.

﴿أَيَحْسَبُ ٱلْإِنسَٰنُ أَن يُتْرَكَ سُدًى ﴿٣٦﴾ أَلَمْ يَكُ نُطْفَةً مِّن مَّنِيٍّ يُمْنَىٰ ﴿٣٧﴾ ثُمَّ كَانَ عَلَقَةً فَخَلَقَ فَسَوَّىٰ ﴿٣٨﴾﴾

"Does man think that he will be left for nothing (without any reckoning)? Was he not (in his beginning) a sperm drop ejaculated (into the woman's womb)? Then it developed into a hanging mass (clinging to the womb like a nest). Then He created (in it the preliminary form of all the limbs of the body). Then He set (them) right."[73]

The human body is in a state of equilibrium; the organs and both the mental and spiritual faculties are perfectly balanced. The question is why has God created this balance? The answer is because this balance allows man to achieve a state of peace, tolerance and security, and through it the faculties of human personality are able to work together in an atmosphere of mutual interaction and co-operation which is conducive to human life.

How can this balance be achieved? God has created in man various facets to his personality; he is a multidimensional being. He has a biological dimension, whilst at the same time he is bound and responsible for the social aspects of his life; he has a spiritual dimension ingrained into his personality whilst at the same time he must deal with the philosophical and intellectual realities of his being. Any imbalance in any of these faculties is regarded as un-Islāmic; Islām recommends its followers fulfil the due requirements of each aspect of human personality so that a balance is achieved; when these requirements are met, peace, tranquillity and tolerance are the final outcome.

---

73 Al-Qur'ān, *al-Qiyāma*, 75: 36-38.

A believer must fulfil the rights of his Creator, the rights of the Prophet (blessings and peace be upon him), the rights of his own person and the rights of society. Progress in one's spiritual life should not occur at the neglect of one's secular obligations, such a monastic approach to life is prohibited in Islām. Similarly, development in one's secular life must not occur at the detriment of one's spiritual and religious needs. Any form of behaviour which has the potential to create an imbalance in ones personality or generate extremist tendencies is prohibited in Islām. We should aim to create a balance within our lives so that when we are confronted by secularists the innate beauty of a believer's secular life shines forth and at the same time the spiritualist should be affected by the believer's spiritual beauty. An example of this is present in the life of the Prophet Muḥammad (blessings and peace be upon him) who interacted with both the young and old and participated in social activities with full vigour.

Tradition notes that the Prophet Muḥammad (blessings and peace be upon him) was actively involved in the popular physical sports of the time, including swimming,[74] horse riding[75] and wrestling,[76] yet at the same time he was a man of great spirituality and in proximity to God. This is the lifestyle that a Muslim must adopt in order to live in harmony with oneself and others. Disapproval of a monastic existence is evident in one tradition when the Prophet (blessings and peace be upon him) enquired a woman about her marriage and relationship to her husband. She

74 Related by Abū Nu'aym in *Ḥilya al-Awliyā'*, vol. 1, p. 184; and al-Hindī in *Kanz al-'Ummāl*, vol. 16, 184 # 45345.

75 Related by al-Bukhārī in *al-Ṣaḥīḥ*, vol. 2, p. 835 # 2242; and vol. 3, pp. 1050, 1332 # 2705, 3446; Muslim in *al-Ṣaḥīḥ*, vol. 2, pp. 680, 681 # 987; and al-Nasā'ī in *al-Sunan*, vol. 6, p. 216 # 3563.

76 Related by Ibn Kathīr in *al-Bidāya wa al-Nihāya*, vol. 3, pp. 103, 104; al-Qasṭallānī in *al-Mawāhib al-Laduniyya*, vol. 2, p. 365; and al-Zurqānī in *Sharḥ al-Mawāhib al-Laduniyya*, vol. 4, p. 292.

responded that he was a very pious individual who would stand the whole night in prayer, and spend the whole day in state of fasting. Upon hearing this, the Prophet (blessings and peace be upon him) rebuked the husband for his conduct,[77] informing him that his wife had rights over him as well as God[78] and that he must fulfil the rights of both in order to live a balanced life.

The same beauty and balance described regarding the human personality is also apparent in the celestial order of the universe. Almighty Allāh has created the whole of this universe on the same principle of balance:

﴿ثُمَّ ٱسْتَوَىٰٓ إِلَى ٱلسَّمَآءِ وَهِىَ دُخَانٌ فَقَالَ لَهَا
وَلِلْأَرْضِ ٱئْتِيَا طَوْعًا أَوْ كَرْهًا قَالَتَآ أَتَيْنَا طَآئِعِينَ ۝١١﴾

"Then He turned towards the heavenly universe — that was (all) smoke. So He said to it (the heavenly spheres) and the earth: "Get in (compliance with Our system) either under the influence of mutual attraction and coordination or under aversion and revulsion." Both said: "We submit with pleasure.""[79]

There is no conflict between the heavens and the earth; the celestial order that has been placed by Almighty Allāh is in a state of balance thereby creating peace. So in the same way that Allāh has provided balance within our human personality and the celestial system around us, it is expected from us, as stewards and trustees of the divine will, to act accordingly with the world around us.

---

77 Related by Aḥmad b. Ḥanbal in *al-Musnad*, vol. 6, p. 226 # 25935; Ibn Ḥibbān in *al-Ṣaḥīḥ*, vol. 1, p. 185 # 9; 'Abd al-Razzāq in *al-Muṣannaf*, vol. 6, pp. 167, 168 # 10375, and vol. 7, p. 150 # 12591; and al-Ṭabarānī in *al-Mu'jam al-Kabir*, vol. 9, p. 38 # 8319.

78 Related by al-Bukhārī in *al-Ṣaḥīḥ*, vol. 2, pp. 696, 697 # 1873, 1874; Muslim in *al-Ṣaḥīḥ*, vol. 2, p. 813 # 1159; and Aḥmad b. Ḥanbal in *al-Musnad*, vol. 2, p. 198.

79 Al-Qur'ān, *Fuṣṣilat*, 41: 11.

These examples simply convey one message: that Islām rejects any kind of extremist tendency in life; regardless of whether extremism is in a positive or negative manner. This then leads to the wondering of how Islām condones terrorism. Acts of terrorism are the result of radicalisation and radicalism is the result of extremism, so if Islām does not allow extremism in one's life then how can it possibly allow terrorism? The causes of terrorism must be investigated and bracketing the Muslim community or Islām with terrorism must be avoided. Terrorism has no link to any religion; it is a social, psychological and economic phenomenon which transcends all barriers of race, religion and culture. Extremists and fanatics have not only existed within Muslims cultures, they have also existed in Western cultures; for this reason every society must search for and uproot all causes and motives which lead to acts of terror.

To further scrutinise Islām's stance on violence and terrorism one need only examine the character and personality of the Prophet Muḥammad (blessings and peace be upon him). When he migrated to Medina a written document was prepared known as the Constitution of Medina; this was one of the first constitutions ever written. The Constitution of Medina formed the basis of a just and peaceful society under the leadership of the Prophet Muḥammad (blessings and peace be upon him) and it was pivotal in the eradication of terrorist and extremist activities that had plagued the Arabian Peninsula for centuries.

At the time there were two major tribes residing in Medina: the Aws and Khazhraj; alongside these two tribes were another eight who were allied to one of them, and thirty-three other groups that existed. In total no less than forty-three different factions existed in Medina when the Prophet (blessings and peace be upon him) migrated there. Through the Constitution of Medina, the Prophet (blessings and peace be upon him) was able to establish a multiethnic and a multicultural society which he administered as the head of state. A fully-fledged charter was provided, which brought about cooperation in aspects of defence, finance, society and politics. Under his leadership, an atmosphere of mutual cooperation was achieved which respected local customary laws; it was an atmosphere which recognised rights for the freedom of religion and culture, with minorities being granted rights to practice their own religion.

One noteworthy example is when a large delegation of Christians from Najrān visited the Prophet (blessings and peace be upon him) in Medina. He received them with great hospitality and allowed them to reside at his Mosque. When they desired to worship, the Prophet (blessings and peace be upon him) offered them the use of his Mosque.[80] The delegation did not come to Medina to have a peaceful dialogue with the Prophet (blessings and peace be upon him) for purposes of mutual understanding. Rather they came with the intention of debating with him to rebut his teachings. This is just one example of who the West must turn to in order to achieve greater understanding of Islāmic teachings.

The sermon delivered by the Prophet (blessings and peace be upon him) during the farewell pilgrimage, is another example of Islām's position on toleration and peace. This sermon was the beginning of a new world order which marked an age grounded in mutual cooperation and peace. The Prophet (blessings and peace be upon him) spoke:

«أَلَا كُلُّ شَيْءٍ مِنْ أَمْرِ الْجَاهِلِيَّةِ تَحْتَ قَدَمَيَّ مَوْضُوعٌ».

---

80 Related by Ibn Sa'd in *al-Ṭabaqāt al-Kubrā*, vol. 1, p. 357; and Ibn al-Qayyim in *Zād al-Ma'ād*, vol. 3, p. 629.

"Be aware! All matters pertaining to the time of age of jāhiliyya (an age of exploitation and oppression) had been trampled under my feet." [81]

This declaration marked the beginning of a new system which was to be based on justice and human dignity; it was a system that was designated to bring about equality amongst mankind. The Prophet (blessings and peace be upon him) continued with,

«إِنَّ دِمَاءَكُمْ وَأَمْوَالَكُمْ حَرَامٌ عَلَيْكُمْ كَحُرْمَةِ يَوْمِكُمْ هَذَا، فِي شَهْرِكُمْ هَذَا، فِي بَلَدِكُمْ هَذَا».

"(O mankind!) Indeed your lives and properties have been sanctified like the sanctity of this holy day, and like the sanctity of this holy month and this holy land of yours." [82]

On the concept of human equality he stated:

«اَلنَّاسُ بَنُو آدَمَ، وَخَلَقَ اللّٰهُ آدَمَ مِنْ تُرَابٍ».

"All mankind is the progeny of Adam and Allāh created Adam from clay." [83]

---

81 Related by Muslim in *al-Ṣaḥīḥ*, vol. 2, p. 889 # 1218; Abū Dāwūd in *al-Sunan*, vol. 2, p. 185 # 1905; Ibn Ḥibbān in *al-Ṣaḥīḥ*, vol. 9, .p. 257 # 3944; al-Nasā'ī in *al-Sunan*, vo. 2, p. 421 # 4001; al-Dārimī in *al-Sunan*, vol. 2, p. 69 # 1850; and Ibn Abī Shayba in *al-Muṣannaf*, vol. 3, p. 336 # 14705.

82 Related by Muslim in *al-Ṣaḥīḥ*, vol. 2, p. 889 # 1218; Abū Dāwūd in *al-Sunan*, vol. 2, p. 185 # 1905; Ibn Ḥibbān in *al-Ṣaḥīḥ*, vol. 9, .p. 257 # 3944; al-Nasā'ī in *al-Sunan*, vo. 2, p. 421 # 4001; al-Dārimī in *al-Sunan*, vol. 2, p. 69 # 1850; and Ibn Abī Shayba in *al-Muṣannaf*, vol. 3, p. 336 # 14705.

83 Related by al-Tirmidhī in *al-Sunan*, vol. 5, p. 389 # 3270; and al-Bayhaqī in *Shu'ab al-Īmān*, vol. 4, p. 286 # 5130.

Furthermore, he stated:

«يَا أَيُّهَا النَّاسُ! أَلَا إِنَّ رَبَّكُمْ وَاحِدٌ، وَإِنَّ أَبَاكُمْ وَاحِدٌ، أَلَا! لَا فَضْلَ لِعَرَبِيٍّ عَلَى أَعْجَمِيٍّ، وَلَا لِعَجَمِيٍّ عَلَى عَرَبِيٍّ، وَلَا لِأَحْمَرَ عَلَى أَسْوَدَ، وَلَا أَسْوَدَ عَلَى أَحْمَرَ إِلَّا بِالتَّقْوَى».

"O People! Be aware! Indeed your Lord is One and your father is one. Be aware! No Arab is superior to a non-Arab, and no non-Arab is superior to an Arab; no red person has a superiority over a black person, and no black person has superiority over a red person, except for those who are God-fearing." [84]

The Qur'ān clarifies this concept in these words:

﴿يَٰٓأَيُّهَا ٱلنَّاسُ إِنَّا خَلَقْنَٰكُم مِّن ذَكَرٍ وَأُنثَىٰ وَجَعَلْنَٰكُمْ شُعُوبًا وَقَبَآئِلَ لِتَعَارَفُوٓاْ ۚ إِنَّ أَكْرَمَكُمْ عِندَ ٱللَّهِ أَتْقَىٰكُمْ ۚ إِنَّ ٱللَّهَ عَلِيمٌ خَبِيرٌ ١٣﴾

"O people! We created you from a male and a female, and (divided) you into (large) peoples and tribes, so that you might recognize one another. Surely the most honourable among you in the sight of Allāh is he who fears Allāh most. Certainly Allāh is All-Knowing, All-Aware." [85]

---

84 Related by Aḥmad b. Ḥanbal in *al-Musnad*, vol. 5, p. 411; Ibn al-Mubārak in *al-Musnad*, p. 147 # 239; and Haythamī in *Majmaʿ al-Zawā'id*, vol. 3, p. 266.

85 Al-Qur'ān, *al-Ḥujurāt*, 49: 13.

The Prophet Muḥammad (blessings and peace be upon him) abolished all falsely concocted superiorities and established the superiority of good character and mindfulness to God. His teachings eradicated economic exploitation and at the same time established the rights of women and the poor. Women were not only granted the right to vote but were also encouraged to take an active role within parliament. In the West, women were not politically enfranchised until the 20th century: it was not until 1920 that women were legally allowed to vote after the 19th amendment to the bill of rights was passed in America;[86] also women were not declared as legal persons until 1929 in Canada. Women had to gain their legal rights gradually in the modern world and Western women have only enjoyed these rights for less than 100 years, whilst Islām provided women with rights instantly without any need of demonstration on their part 1400 hundred years ago.

In the days of the Caliph 'Umar b. al-Khaṭṭāb (may Allāh be well pleased with him), a motion was being discussed which limited the amount a women could receive in dower. During this discussion a women stood up and criticised the bill, objecting that God did not limit the dower so why should 'Umar; when asked for evidence for her claims she recited the following Qur'ānic verse:

﴿وَإِنْ أَرَدتُّمُ ٱسْتِبْدَالَ زَوْجٍ مَّكَانَ زَوْجٍ
وَءَاتَيْتُمْ إِحْدَىٰهُنَّ قِنطَارًا فَلَا تَأْخُذُوا۟ مِنْهُ شَيْـًٔا
ۚ أَتَأْخُذُونَهُۥ بُهْتَـٰنًا وَإِثْمًا مُّبِينًا ﴿٢٠﴾﴾

86 Hart, James, The American Presidency in Action 1789: A Study in Constitutional History, New York, The Macmillan Company, 1948; Melvin I. Urofsky, Paul Finkelman, A March of Liberty: A Constitutional History of the United States (two volumes), Oxford University Press, 2002.

> *"And if you seek to take a wife in place of another and you have (by now) given to her heaps of wealth, yet do not take back any part of it. Do you want to take that wealth (back) by means of unjust accusation and manifest sin?"* [87]

The objection of the woman suggests that she was a member of the parliament and therefore had both legal and political rights. When 'Umar (may Allāh be well pleased with him) heard this evidence he quickly withdrew his bill and stated that the woman was correct and he was wrong.[88]

At the practical level, democracy was revived by the Prophet Muḥammad (blessings and peace be upon him) who established local governance in Medina. He ordered a society in which a group of ten people was headed by a councillor known as an *'ārif*, and a group of ten *'ārif* was headed by a deputy known as the *naqīb*; the *naqīb* was a member of the parliament of Medina. So every 100 persons in society were represented in parliament by their *naqīb*. Despite being the representative of God on earth, the Prophet Muḥammad (blessings and peace be upon him), transferred power to the common member of society; this was a practical demonstration of consultative democracy in the life of the Prophet which characterised true Islāmic societies.

In the Modern world certain Western nations, in the name of high principles, terrorise weaker nations into submitting to their own concocted regulations and dictums. Democracy, human rights and liberty are being redefined; the concept of sovereignty is being changed and diminished to fulfil the whims of the powerful. This uni-polar hegemony seeks to create a monopoly over the world dictating its own terms and conditions. If we are to revive peace in our world today we have to revive the concept of

---

87 Al-Qur'ān, *al-Nisā'*, 4: 20.

88 Related by 'Abd ar-Razzāq in *al-Muṣannaf*, vol. 6, p. 180 # 10420; and al-Shawkānī in *Nayl al-Awṭār*, vol. 6, p. 314.

multiculturalism; we must accept diversity in the world and not expect others to be subjected to our own criterions and customs. As demonstrated by the aforementioned evidences returning to Islām is the only true viable means of achieving peace, as it champions the rights of every nation and enjoins multiculturalism and diversity.

4. A DETAILED EXPOSITION OF THE MEANINGS OF *JIHĀD*: A REFUTATION OF MISINTERPRETATIONS

Another important aspect of Islām which has been manipulated is the concept of Jihād and the misconceptions surrounding it need to be removed. This term has become popular amongst Muslims and non-Muslims alike but unfortunately it is confronted with misunderstandings on both sides. The word *jihād* comes from the word *juhd* which means 'to struggle';[89] it does not denote killing or warfare. It is a struggle for a greater good, for the betterment of mankind; it is a tool of eliminating oppression and terror; it is a means to an end, not an end within itself. The ultimate end of *jihād* is the establishment of peace at all levels. It is interesting to note that *jihād* is not monolithic: it is of various kinds and categories. The best *jihād*, and the greatest *jihād* in status, is *jihād bi'n-nafs*: to struggle against one's ego.

The Holy Prophet (blessings and peace be upon him) said:

«الْمُجَاهِدُ مَنْ جَاهَدَ نَفْسَهُ».

89 Ibn Fāras, *Mu'jam Maqāyīs al-Lugha*, p. 210; Abū Manṣūr al-Azhārī, *Tahdhīb al-Lugha*, vol. 6, p. 26, Rāghib al-Aṣfahānī, *al-Mufradāt*, p. 101; Ibn Manẓūr, *Lisān al-'Arab*, vol. 3, p. 143.

"Mujahid is the one who fights against the wrong propensities of his Self."[90]

After returning from a battle with his Companions (may Allāh be well pleased with them), the Prophet (blessings and peace be upon him) stated:

«قَدِمْتُمْ مِنَ الْجِهَادِ الْأَصْغَرِ إِلَى الْجِهَادِ الْأَكْبَرِ».

"You have come from the smaller jihād to the greater jihād."[91]

The struggle against the self is a means of disciplining one's self from the evil propensities of the soul, such as sexual desires, material greed, lust for power and all other impure wishes. Islām does not aim to eliminate these completely but through self-discipline it aims to bring them under control; in this way Islām provides a means to organise one's life appropriately. This process of disciplining the soul is known as *tazkiya*, self-purification, which can be achieved by constant remembrance of Almighty Allāh.

In Medina the Prophet (blessings and peace be upon him) used to provide an atmosphere for the Companions (may Allāh be well pleased with them) for the greater *jihād* by conducting gatherings in the remembrance of Allāh for the purification of the soul.

The second *jihād* is *jihād bi'l-'ilm*: the struggle for attaining and propagating knowledge. The Prophet (blessings and peace be upon

---

90 Related by al-Tirmidhī in *al-Sunan*, vol. 4, p. 165 # 1621; Ibn Ḥibbān in *al-Ṣaḥīḥ*, vol. 10, p. 484 # 4624; al-Ḥākim in *al-Mustadrak*, vol. 2, p. 156 # 2637; al-Bazzār in *al-Musnad*, vol. 2, p. 156 # 3753; and al-Ṭabarānī in *al-Mu'jam al-Kabīr*, vol. 18, p. 256 # 641.

91 Related by al-Khaṭīb al-Baghdādī, in *Tārīkh Baghdād*, vol. 13, p. 523; Ibn 'Asākir in *Tārīkh Dimashq al-Kabīr*, vol. 6, p. 438; Ibn Rajab al-Ḥanbalī in *Jāmi' al-'Ulūm wa al-Hikam*, vol. 1, p. 196; and al-Mizzī in *Tahdhīb al-Kamāl*, vol. 2, p. 144.

him) told his Companions (may Allāh be well pleased with them) that if he were to choose between a group of people engaged in the remembrance of Allāh and the other in the propagation of knowledge, he would choose the group engaged in the attainment of knowledge. Thus the remembrance of Allāh and the seeking of knowledge are declared the highest forms of *jihād* in Islām. This is why the first revelation of *Islām* was a revelation concerning the acquisition of knowledge. The Qur'ān states:

﴿ٱقْرَأْ بِٱسْمِ رَبِّكَ ٱلَّذِى خَلَقَ ۝١ خَلَقَ ٱلْإِنسَـٰنَ مِنْ عَلَقٍ ۝٢ ٱقْرَأْ وَرَبُّكَ ٱلْأَكْرَمُ ۝٣ ٱلَّذِى عَلَّمَ بِٱلْقَلَمِ ۝٤ عَلَّمَ ٱلْإِنسَـٰنَ مَا لَمْ يَعْلَمْ ۝٥﴾

"(O Beloved!) Read (commencing) with the Name of Allāh, Who has created (everything). He created man from a hanging mass (clinging) like a leech (in the mother's womb). Read and your Lord is Most Generous, Who taught man (reading and writing) by the pen, Who (besides that) taught man (all that) which he did not know."[92]

Likewise, propagating the religion and calling others to the way of Islām is also a *jihād* which is known as *da'wa*.

Jihād bi'l-'aml is the third kind of *jihād* which encourages people to do righteous deeds for the uplifting of morality; that you struggle for the promotion of spirituality, and guarding human values for the betterment of society.

The fourth is *jihād bi'l-māl*: it is the *jihād* of charity and that one spends their money to help the poor and needy.

Finally, the last kind of *jihād* is *jihād bi'l-qitāl*, which is the *jihād* of just-war (war for defence instead of just-war). After knowing this it would be unjust to concentrate on this form of *jihād* at the

[92] Al-Qur'ān, *al-'Alaq*, 96: 1-5.

exclusion of the rest. Furthermore, for this *jihād* to take place there are strict criterions and conditions. It was essentially legislated for the defence of one's rights, to defend humanity from all forms of oppression and aggression. In the same way that the UN permits countries to wage war to eliminate oppression and aggression, Islām allows *jihād* to be waged for the very same reasons.

Interestingly, *jihād bi'l-qitāl* was never commanded in the first nineteen years of the promulgation of Islām. The Prophet spent thirteen years in Makkah and was never commanded to fight. In Medina there was no commandment for *jihād bi'l-qitāl* for the first six years; whatever warfare was conducted in that time was purely committed out of self-defence and were fought near the boundaries of Medina. It was not until after the treaty of Ḥudaybiya that the Muslims were permitted to wage an offensive war against the enemies of humanity and mankind to eliminate terrorism and oppression. Almost two decades were spent in either peaceful preaching or self-defence until offensive warfare, *jihād bi 'l-qitāl*, was permitted for Muslims. The Qur'ān states:

﴿أُذِنَ لِلَّذِينَ يُقَٰتَلُونَ بِأَنَّهُمْ ظُلِمُوا۟ ۚ وَإِنَّ ٱللَّهَ

عَلَىٰ نَصْرِهِمْ لَقَدِيرٌ ﴿٣٩﴾﴾

"Permission (to fight against mischief, disruption and oppression) is granted to those against whom (unjust) war is waged, because they were oppressed and Allāh is doubtlessly All-Powerful to help them (the oppressed)."[93]

It is important to understand that *jihād bi'l-qitāl* is based on the concept of peace and is only permitted when all other forms of reconciliations have failed. Islām forbids one to either kill or maim

---

93 Al-Qur'ān, *al-Ḥajj*, 22: 39.

any non-combatant;[94] doing so is considered a war crime. During warfare one is not allowed to kill or wound worshippers who may be residing within a monastery or place of worship. Buildings cannot be destroyed or trees; and any kind of disturbances for the local population is totally forbidden.[95] Engaging in a conflict that contradicts any of these conditions would nullify the just cause of one's struggle, and one would be sinful in the eyes of God, as the purpose of *jihād bi'l-qitāl* is to bring about peace.

The Prophet's Companion and the first rightly-guided Caliph Abū Bakr (may Allāh be well pleased with him) would issue written and verbal instructions to the Muslim army to honour the above injunctions during a war.[96]

The notion that Islām was spread by the sword is false; it has always spread peacefully through the integrity of its character and teachings, as attested by Phillip K. Hitti in his *History of the Arabs*. It is strange that today amongst the Muslims there is an unrestrained zeal to declare war against 'infidels' by misusing and abusing the term *jihād*. Such people have no understanding of what *jihād* means, instead they are fuelled by their egos and desires. They have no commitment to keeping to the strict guidelines set by our pious predecessors. As a result they create a greater loss and damage for Muslims, thereby exacerbating the problems that already exist.

---

94 Related by Muslim in *al-Ṣaḥīḥ*, vol. 3, p. 1407 # 1780; Abū Dāwūd in *al-Sunan*, vol. 3, p. 162 # 3021; and al-Bazzār in *al-Musnad*, vol. 4, p. 122 # 1292.

95 Related by Aḥmad b. Ḥanbal in *al-Musnad*, vol. 5, p. 385 # 2728; Ibn Abī Shayba in *al-Muṣannaf*, vol. 6, pp. 483, 484 # 33127, 33132; Abū Ya'lā in *al-Musnad*, vol. 5, p. 59 # 2650; al-Ṭaḥāwī in *Sharḥ Ma'ānī al-Āthār*, vol. 3, p. 225; al-Bayhaqī in *al-Sunan al-Kubrā*, vol. 9, pp. 85, 90 # 17904, 17929; and al-Daylamī in *Musnad al-Firdaws*, vol. 5, p. 45 # 7410.

96 Related by al-Tirmidhī in *al-Sunan*, vol. 4, p. 122 # 1552; al-Mālik in *al-Mawaṭṭā*, vol. 2, p. 447 # 965; 'Abd al-Razzāq in *al-Muṣannaf*, vol. 5, p. 199 # 9375; Ibn Abī Shayba in *al-Muṣannaf*, vol. 6, p. 483 # 33121; al-Bayhaqī in *al-Sunan al-Kubrā*, vol. 9, pp. 89, 90 # 17927, 17929; and al-Mirwazī in *Musnad Abī Bakr*, pp. 69-72 # 21.

It is a well known principle that if there is a clear indication that if going into conflict one's enemy will become triumphant and much damage will be exacted on the Muslims, or that there is a great danger of irreparable damage on behalf of the Muslims, then going to war is prohibited. *Islām* also discourages Muslims from entering into a battle with their enemy if they are not adequately equipped. One tradition narrates that a group of Companions (may Allāh be well pleased with them) of the Prophet Muḥammad (blessings and peace be upon him) went to war in the Arabian Peninsula. Upon realising that they were outnumbered and that if they advanced towards their enemy they faced defeat, they retreated back to Medina. They informed the Prophet (blessings and peace be upon him), telling him *naḥn al-farrārūn, yā Rasūl Allāh,* 'We are ones who fled (from the battlefield) O Messenger of Allāh.' The Prophet (blessings and peace be upon him) replied, *lā, bal antum al-'akkārūn,* 'No, in fact you are the ones who returned safely.'[97]

And through these words they were consoled. This shows that if one advances to war and there is a chance of irreparable loss and damage, then fighting no longer becomes obligatory, but prohibited, and it becomes necessary to avoid fighting in order to curb the possibility of long-term damage. Therefore a call to *jihād* in the Muslim modern world is a far cry from the noble practice of our ancestors and in no way can it be justified.

5. ORIGIN OF MODERN "MUSLIM" TERRORIST GROUPS

Aside from Muslims themselves painting a distorted image of Islām it is quite apparent that the West, in recent years, has grown

---

97 Related by Abū Dāwūd in *al-Sunan*, vol. 3, p. 46 # 2647; al-Tirmidhī in *al-Sunan*, vol. 4, p. 215 # 1716; Aḥmad b. Ḥanbal in *al-Musnad*, vol. 2, pp. 70, 100, 110; and al-Bayhaqī in *al-Sunan al-Kubrā*, vol. 9, p. 76 # 17861, 17862.

hostile towards the Muslim world. There seems to be a twofold strategy against the Muslims: the first is a biased coverage in the mainstream media which not only creates misgivings about Islām and Muslims but also adds to the propaganda that Islām is a fascist and extremist religion, averse to peace and cooperation; and the second is their covert assistance of extremist and terrorist groups through funding and training. One only needs to open the books of international history to find out when these groups received their initial training and support: the establishment of terrorist networks and their proliferation in Central Asia came at the hands of the powerful Western nations for the sole purpose of advancing their national self interest in opposition to the Soviet Union. This is the kind of double-faced policy that the West exhibits vis-à-vis the Muslims world. If it was not for this handful of terrorists, military intervention and occupation could not be legitimised without it being dubbed as neo-colonialism. Therefore, not until the powerful nations abandon the path of extremism, terrorism in the world cannot be eliminated; we must aim to tackle the root cause of the problem, not its symptoms.

Firstly the West's betrayal of the Muslim world is a case in point. The dual policies that the West exhibits towards the Muslim world through the defunct organisation known as the UN must be addressed. The sanctity of life should be upheld for all people regardless of their race, creed or colour.

6. HISTORIC EXISTENCE OF EXTREMISTS AND TERRORISTS IN THE FORM OF THE KHAWARIJITE

Within the Muslim community where a minority has left the path of balance and moderation the duty is upon the majority to reclaim the beautiful religion of Islām from the extremists; we cannot allow them to speak in our name. The extremists have adopted a twofold strategy to target the youth: intellectually or militantly. The former is related to the Zahirite ideology, whilst the latter is related to the Khawarijite. The Muslim youths must take great precaution for they are most vulnerable and most likely to be preyed upon. The Zahirite ideology has been absolutely rejected by the majority of Muslims throughout history: this ideology exacted a literalist interpretation of the Qur'ān and Sunna and they did not go beyond the letter of the law. In time they lost sight of the aims and objectives of the Sharī'a and had lost the spirit of the law. They sought to fulfil the legal rulings of the Sharī'a but neglected its wisdom, and so within time their school became inept and their influence was wiped away from Muslim societies.

The Zahirites went against the verse of the Qur'ān in which Allāh states:

﴿وَيُعَلِّمُكُمُ ٱلْكِتَـٰبَ وَٱلْحِكْمَةَ﴾.

"And he teaches you the Book and inculcates in you logic and wisdom."[98]

Understanding the wisdom behind the text is paramount for the correct application of the Sharī'a in the world. In matters of worship and spirituality the rulings remain predominantly the same, but as for matters concerning the secular aspect of one's life there is a need to understand the wisdom behind the rulings, because as things change and new situations arise the rulings change in order to make the Sharī'a fully adept to the environment in which it is practiced; and, as we have seen, the Zahirite ideology which refused to adapt and reconstruct itself became outmoded and unfit for society, it lost adherents and

98 Al-Qur'ān, *al-Baqara*, 2: 151.

became extinct. This dynamic spirit of reconstruction is the concept of *ijtihād*, which vitalises the spirit of the Sharīʿa making it practicable in every age and society. This is what a qualified *mujtahid* does: he interprets the texts and applies it appropriately according to the dictates of time and place. In no way does this mean that the Sharīʿa is subjugated to the whims and fancies of men, but rather the *mujtahid* who seeks to apply the spirit of the Sharīʿa earnestly strives to stay true to the letter of the law to the best of his ability. Thus Islām in this sense is not a static and outmoded religion, but rather it is dynamic.

As for the Khawarijites, Muslim history bears testimony to their unorthodoxy and heresy. They were declared as outcasts by the Prophet and the Orthodox Caliphs. In fact they *fought* against the fourth orthodox Caliph, ʿAlī al-Murtaḍā (may Allāh be well pleased with him). They were narrow-minded and possessed a short-sighted understanding of their religion and life in general. Their hallmark was that they were equipped with the best slogans and had a tendency to declare others as disbelievers and infidels. They were the most vocal for the implementation of the Sharīʿa and for establishing God's rule on earth; so when Ali, the fourth Orthodox Caliph of Islām, accepted mediation during the battle of Ṣiffīn, the Khawarijites were quick to condemn him for what they believed was a compromise of God's rule and declared him an infidel.[99] Their slogan was *ini'l-ḥukm illā li-Allāh*: 'there is no rule except for God's.' ʿAlī al-Murtaḍā (may Allāh be well pleased with him), when asked about this slogan, replied:

---

[99] For complete details, see: Qadri, Tahir-ul., Fatwa on Suicide Bombings and Terrorism. United Kingdom: Bodmin and King's Lynn, 2010.

«كَلِمَةُ حَقٍّ أُرِيْدَ بِهَا بَاطِلٌ».

"That is true but the intentions behind it are invalid."[100]

We can see the remnants of the Khawarijite legacy amongst the youths who have become frustrated with the frequent mishaps in the Muslim world. The attacks against their Muslim identity, be it within Western society as exhibited in the Salman Rushdie case or in the Muslim world through the systematic oppression of Muslim people, has left them emotionally frustrated and angered; as a result they vent their anger through the extremist groups who they feel are the only ones addressing the issues. Thus slogans such as Sharī'a for the UK; behead those who insult Islām; *jihād* is our way; freedom of speech go to hell, are all manifestations of this Khawarijite tendency that has re-emerged amongst young Muslims due to their emotional frustration. However this minority possesses no legitimate religious authority and is completely alien to the teachings and wisdoms of Islām.

7. PROPHETIC BIOGRAPHY (*SĪRA*) AS A MODEL FOR THE UMMA'S SUCCESS

For the Muslims, success will now only emerge if they retract to the *sīra* of the Prophet Muḥammad (blessings and peace be upon him). His life can be divided into three stages: the first stage in Makkah and two significant stages in Medina.

The Prophet (blessings and peace be upon him) spent the first thirteen years of his life in Makkah, teaching the early Muslims about strengthening one's faith and building upon one's morality,

100 Related by Muslim in *al-Ṣaḥīḥ*, vol. 2, p. 749 # 1066; al-Nasā'ī in *al-Sunan al-Kubrā*, vol. 5, p. 160 # 8562; Ibn Abī Shayba in *al-Muṣannaf*, vol. 7, p. 557 # 37907; and al-Bayhaqī in *al-Sunan al-Kubrā*, vol. 8, p.171 # 16478.

ethics and spirituality. Through the firmness of faith, Islām was spread, this period was therefore characterised with the advancement of knowledge. Thereafter the Prophet (blessings and peace be upon him) migrated to Medina and this migration heralded the second phase. In the six or seven years of the first Medinan phase there was a greater concentration upon the building of the Muslim state. Its initiation was characterised by a social contract known as the *muwākhāt,* which brought together warring tribes under a unified banner. During these years efforts were made for the social and economical stability of the newly formed community: steps were taken by the Prophet (blessings and peace be upon him) for the elimination of poverty in order to grant the citizens of the society with economic stability and prosperity; he made all Muslim brothers to one another and distributed their wealth amongst them so that all economic deadlocks may be resolved; they would share their earnings and holdings so that they would become economically strong to stave off any potential threat or enemy.

As a result of the Constitution of Medina Prophet Muḥammad (blessings and peace be upon him) created peace between the various tribes and also brought the Jewish tribes into the treaty. The Jews were fully integrated into the Muslim community. However, with the passage of time, as the Muslims gained both economical and political strength the Jews broke off their alliance. During these six years, it was clear that relations between the Jews and Muslims would not last; Allāh informed the Muslims in the Qur'ān about their hostility, but the Prophet (blessings and peace be upon him) did not fight against them lest he would be confronted by two powerful enemies at the same time: the polytheist of Makkah in the south and the Jews of Khaybar in the north. And indeed the Muslims were attacked.

The Prophet (blessings and peace be upon him) knew of these developments so he set out to Makkah with his Companions (may

Allāh be well pleased with them) for the Hajj pilgrimage. When the Makkans prevented him and his followers from entering the city he signed a ten-year no-war pact which historically became known as the 'Treaty of Hudaybiya.' The Treaty of Hudaybiya marked the beginning of the third phase of the *sīra* of the Prophet (blessings and peace be upon him): As a result of the treaty he, through his wisdom, prevented his enemies from attacking him from the south whilst he dealt with his enemies from the north; by doing so he avoided the Muslims from fighting a double fronted battle. At the time of signing the treaty the companions were not aware of its inherent wisdom: the majority of the clauses were actually not in favour of the Muslims and were heavily biased towards the Makkans, giving them privileges at the expense of the Muslims. But despite the unevenness of this treaty, the Prophet (blessings and peace be upon him) signed it and told the companions to be patient for it heralded a truly great victory.

Being barred from entry into Makka and not being allowed to perform Ḥajj that year, the Holy Prophet (blessings and peace be upon him) ordered the Companions (may Allāh be well pleased with them) to get ready for a pre-emptive attack. With the polytheists bound from the south the Muslims were safe to dispose of their enemies in the north; the result was a decisive victory for the Muslims: Khaybar had been conquered. This victory turned the tide and made Islām the most powerful force in the Arabian Peninsula.

For nineteen years the Holy Prophet (blessings and peace be upon him) and the Muslims remained patient with their enemies: the first thirteen years were characterised by non-violence and non-retaliations whilst the latter six years were of self-defence.

8. CLOSING WORDS: THE TRUE WAY FORWARD FOR MUSLIMS

So what steps should we take? First and foremost Muslims must strengthen themselves spiritually, morally and ethically, reviving the culture of learning and academia and strengthening technologically and scientifically. Then, following the precedent of the Holy Prophet (blessings and peace be upon him) in Medina, the Muslim world should strengthen itself economically and bring their resources together in a way similar to the EU which began its journey from a European 'economic community' to a 'United States of Europe'. The Muslim world cannot be revived politically unless it alleviates poverty and bears in mind this current mono-polar world is not a stable one and that a multi-polar world is bound to emerge. The next poles of global polar will be Europe, Russia and the South Pacific Rim including Japan and China. The Muslim world consists of fifty-six countries and can become a block of power if it has the will, but only if it strengthens itself both scientifically and technologically. Once consolidated, it will have the power to choose who it aligns itself with: Europe, Russia, or the South Pacific Rim and it can then ultimately present itself as equals in the world.

- PART 3A -
ISLAM, PEACE AND DEMOCRACY

[Editor's Note: The following is a short discourse. It was delivered to a large western audience including a delegate of guests comprised of a Christian Representative, University Professors, Researchers, a Journalist, and a Civil Servant. Their questions are featured below.]

1. INTRODUCTION

ISLĀM IS A RELIGION OF PEACE AND DEMOCRACY; it is my intention to explore this aspect of Islām using Islām's first written Constitution. It was drafted by the Holy Prophet Muḥammad (blessings and peace be upon him) when he was declared head of the state of Medina.

2. ETYMOLOGY OF THE ARABIC WORD *ISLĀM*

Let us start by exploring the root word of Islām. The root word of Islām is *silm* and *salama*, which means to come into peace and to provide others with peace.[101]

The Qur'ān states:

﴿يَـٰٓأَيُّهَا ٱلَّذِينَ ءَامَنُوا۟ ٱدْخُلُوا۟ فِى ٱلسِّلْمِ كَآفَّةً﴾.

101 Ibn Manẓūr, *Lisān al-'Arab*, vol. 12, p. 289; Rāghib al-Aṣfahānī, *al-Mufradāt*, pp. 239, 240.

"O believers! Enter Islam perfectly and wholly."[102]

Any act, policy, or stance which is against the peace of mankind is considered an un-Islāmic activity. This concept of Islām was practiced and propagated by the Holy Prophet Muḥammad (blessings and peace be upon him). In order to elucidate this concept further, I would like to present the life of the Holy Prophet Muḥammad (blessings and peace be upon him) as an archetype which will serve as a practical demonstration and an exegesis of Allāh's commandment of adopting peace in its entirety.

3. SEVEN POINT SOCIAL POLICY FORMULATED BY THE HOLY PROPHET

Before the Prophet (blessings and peace be upon him) decided to emigrate from Makkah to Medina, a gathering took place in Minā (near Makkah). The gathering formed what was to be known as the first pledge of allegiance; the *bay'a al-'aqaba al-'ūlā*. Twelve people from Medina came to see the Holy Prophet Muḥammad (blessings and peace be upon him) and embraced Islām. Thereafter they made a hand-in-hand pledge with the Holy Prophet (blessings and peace be upon him), affirming their loyalty and allegiance to him. During this meeting, the Prophet (blessings and peace be upon him) delivered a sermon and introduced Islām to them which was to be their very first lesson on the religion. Later, the twelve delegates were appointed by the Holy Prophet (blessings and peace be upon him) as his representatives; to propagate and introduce Islām to the society of Medina.[103]

---

102 Al-Qur'ān, *al-Baqara*, 2: 208.

103 Related by al-Bukhārī in *al-Ṣaḥīḥ*, vol. 1, p. 15 # 18; Aḥmad b. Ḥanbal in *al-Musnad*, vol. 5, p. 323; Ibn Hishām in *al-Sīra al-Nabawiyya*, vol. 6, p. 281; al-Ṭabarī in *Tārīkh al-Umam wa al-Mulūk*, vol. 1, p. 559; Ibn Kathīr in *al-Bidāya wa al-Nihāya*, vol. 3, pp. 150, 151; and Ibn Khaldūn in his well-known *History*, vol. 2, p. 348.

This first sermon consisted of seven points, and through these points the Prophet (blessings and peace be upon him) laid down his vision of a good society. The first point of this sermon was a commandment of faith and obedience to Almighty Allāh - the Lord and Creator. The second point, after belief in the creator and submission to Him, was the prohibition of theft. The third point was that there should be no adultery or fornication in one's life, so that one is free from all sexual immoralities and crimes. Fourth, there should be no killing, particularly of females and mankind in general. Fifth, there should be no false allegations or false accusations against anyone. Sixth, that there should be no back-biting. Finally, the seventh point was the obligation to practice and propagate the good and to abstain from evil. The delegate returned to Medina with this message of Islām. All basic books of Islāmic history have narrated this sermon undisputedly. So this is not any isolated tradition, but a very famous and unanimously agreed-upon tradition.

Note, that only one point (out of the seven) is related to the religious and spiritual message of Islām. The rest are related to the reformation and refinement of man's moral ethics and conduct, and are all secular in nature. The Prophet's main emphasis was to protect human life in its individual sphere, as well as in its collective sphere, from all kinds of social crimes and injustices.

4. THE FIRST PUBLIC FRIDAY ADDRESS DELIVERED BY THE HOLY PROPHET TO THE PEOPLE OF MEDINA

When the Holy Prophet (blessings and peace be upon him) eventually migrated from Makkah to Medina, he delivered his first public Friday lecture in Masjid al-Jumu'a [*Mosque*], as recorded by the authorities of Islāmic history.[104] This extended Friday lecture became his first official public address directed at the inhabitants of Medina. A point of note here is that although the Holy Prophet (blessings and peace be upon him) was personally in great trouble and difficulty; forced to leave his beloved homeland Makkah due to the Makkans' oppression and cruelty towards him, he never once mentioned a single aspect of their misconduct towards him in his address. A diligent observer will recognise that the Prophet (blessings and peace be upon him) came to Medina specifically determined in setting up a just and democratic society based on Islāmic ideals and morals.

Like the sermon on the day of the first pledge of allegiance, the first sermon addressed to the citizens of Medina by the Holy Prophet (blessings and peace be upon him), was the lesson of worship and obedience to Almighty Allāh. In it he also emphasised truthfulness and mutual love amongst everyone, to fulfil promises and commitments, and finally to differentiate and discriminate between the lawful and unlawful in one's life with piety and God-wariness, so that nobody is harmed by one's actions and conduct. Again, the whole of this lecture consisted of a policy of social reform; a policy based on human rights, human dignity, and mutual brotherhood.

104 Related by al-Ṭabarī in *Tārīkh al-Umam wa al-Mulūk*, vol. 2, pp. 7, 8; Ibn al-Jawzī in *al-Muntaẓam fī Tārīkh al-Mulūk wa al-Umam*, vol. 3, pp. 65-67; al-Qurṭubī in *al-Jāmi' li-Aḥkām al-Qur'ān*, vol. 18, pp. 98-100; and Ibn Kathīr in *al-Bidāya wa al-Nihāya*, vol. 3, pp. 212-214.

5. BRIEF EXAMINATION OF THE CONSTITUTION DELIVERED BY THE HOLY PROPHET

[Editors Note:, This was arguably the first written constitution in Human History. A historical social and political manoeuvre which became the basis for the development of democracy. For more information see Shaykh-ul-Islam's books: *The Pact of Medina*; *Muqaddima Sīra al-Rasūl (blessings and peace be upon him)*.]

After briefly glossing over these two sermons of the Holy Prophet (blessings and peace be upon him), I would like to turn your attention to a Constitution gifted to humanity by the Holy Prophet (blessings and peace be upon him), which was known as *al-Ṣaḥīfa*, or the 'Constitution of Medina'. This Constitution brought within its jurisdictions the local Muslim inhabitants of Medina, the emigrants of Makkah, the local Jewish community and other non-Muslim tribes, as well as their allies. The Constitution delineated the constitutional foundation of the Madinian society; it provided the concept of devolution of powers which materialised into democracy in the practical sense. Through the Constitution, a moderate and balanced aptitude was formulated towards all communities regardless of their faith or ethnicity. The concept of a unified, geographical and territorial nation, which included Muslims and non-Muslims alike, which brought together various faiths and cultures as a single whole, was advanced by the Holy Prophet (blessings and peace be upon him). Likewise, the supremacy of the rule of law was also articulated through the Constitution coupled with respect for local customs and laws. The tradition of all local tribes under the rule of law, and protection of culture and religion was advocated. Through the Constitution, the Holy Prophet (blessings and peace be upon him) postulated basic human rights thereby introducing the concept of protection of religious freedom of minorities, and the protection of their culture and religion. The Holy Prophet (blessings and peace be upon him) declared the state of Medina as a sanctuary of peace and security; no act of oppression, injustice, or extremism would be allowed in the state of Medina.

The Constitution begins with the Holy Prophet (blessings and peace be upon him) declaring the Muslims and non-Muslims and their allies from the Jews, as a single nation united together. In this declaration he did not exclude non-Muslims from being part of the Medinan community, as he was unanimously accepted as the head of state.

5.1 OPENING ARTICLES

Article 1 states:

«هَذَا كِتَابٌ مِنْ مُحَمَّدٍ النَّبِيِّ ﷺ».

"This is a constitutional document given by Muḥammad, the Prophet."[105]

The subsequent article, states:

«بَيْنَ الْمُؤْمِنِينَ وَالْمُسْلِمِينَ مِنْ قُرَيْشٍ وَيَثْرِب،

وَمَنْ تَبِعَهُمْ فَلَحِقَ بِهِمْ وَجَاهَدَ مَعَهُمْ».

"(This shall be a pact) between the Muslims of Quraysh, the people of Yathrib (the citizens of Medina), and those who shall follow them and

---

105 Related by Ibn Hishām in *al-Sīra al-Nabawiyya*, vol. 3, p. 31; Abū 'Ubayd al-Qāsim in *Kitāb al-Amwāl*, vol. 1, p. 260; Ibn Zanjuway in *Kitāb al-Amwāl*, p. 205; Ibn Taymiyya in *al-Ṣārim al-Maslūl*, p. 62; Ibn Kathīr in *al-Bidāya wa al-Nihāya*, vol. 2, p. 260; Ibn Sayyid al-Nās, vol. 1, p. 227; and al-Ṣāliḥī in *Subul al-Hudā wa al-Rishād*, vol. 3, p. 382.

become attached to them (politically) and fight along with them (i.e. All of these communities shall be the constitutional subjects of the state)."[106]

And, article 3 confirms:

«إِنَّهُمْ أُمَّةٌ وَاحِدَةٌ مِنْ دُونِ النَّاسِ».

"The aforementioned communities shall formulate a constitutional unity as distinct from (other) people."[107]

The Constitution's opening articles state that Muslims of Quraysh and Yathrib, and those who followed and joined them, are of one community. The policies of the new Medinian State assert that the immigrant Muslims of Makkah and native Muslims of Medina constitute one community. The Constitution established a free Islāmic State on the principles of equality, equity, and religious freedom.

5.2 FREEDOM OF RELIGION

An entire chapter of the Qur'ān which guarantees man's religious freedom even if it is contrary to Muslim beliefs demonstrates the highest possible form of religious tolerance.

The Qur'ān states in the chapter of *al-Kāfirūn* (the disbelievers):

---

106 Related by Ibn Hishām in *al-Sīra al-Nabawiyya*, vol. 3, p. 32; Abū 'Ubayd al-Qāsim in *Kitāb al-Amwāl*, vol. 1, p. 260; Ibn Zanjuway in *Kitāb al-Amwāl*, p. 205; al-Bayhaqī in *al-Sunan al-Kubrā*, vol. 8, p. 106; Ibn Taymiyya in *al-Ṣārim al-Maslūl*, p. 62; Ibn al-Qayyim in *Aḥkām Ahl al-Dhimma*, vol. 3, p. 1405; Ibn Kathīr in *al-Bidāya wa al-Nihāya*, vol. 2, p. 260; Ibn Sayyid al-Nās, vol. 1, p. 227; al-Suhaylī in *al-Rawḍ al-Unuf*, vol. 2, p. 349; and al-Ṣāliḥī in *Subul al-Hudā wa al-Rishād*, vol. 3, p. 382.

107 Related by Ibn Hishām in *al-Sīra al-Nabawiyya*, vol. 3, p. 32; Abū 'Ubayd al-Qāsim in *Kitāb al-Amwāl*, vol. 1, p. 260; Ibn Zanjuway in *Kitāb al-Amwāl*, p. 205; al-Bayhaqī in *al-Sunan al-Kubrā*, vol. 8, p. 106; Ibn Taymiyya in *al-Ṣārim al-Maslūl*, p. 63; Ibn al-Qayyim in *Aḥkām Ahl al-Dhimma*, vol. 3, p. 1405; Ibn Kathīr in *al-Bidāya wa al-Nihāya*, vol. 2, p. 260; Ibn Sayyid al-Nās, vol. 1, p. 227; al-Suhaylī in *al-Rawḍ al-Unuf*, vol. 2, p. 349; and al-Ṣāliḥī in *Subul al-Hudā wa al-Rishād*, vol. 3, p. 382.

﴿قُلْ يَـٰٓأَيُّهَا ٱلْكَـٰفِرُونَ ۝١ لَآ أَعْبُدُ مَا تَعْبُدُونَ ۝٢ وَلَآ أَنتُمْ عَـٰبِدُونَ مَآ أَعْبُدُ ۝٣ وَلَآ أَنَا۠ عَابِدٌ مَّا عَبَدتُّمْ ۝٤ وَلَآ أَنتُمْ عَـٰبِدُونَ مَآ أَعْبُدُ ۝٥ لَكُمْ دِينُكُمْ وَلِىَ دِينِ ۝٦﴾.

"Say: 'O disbelievers! I do not worship those (idols) that you worship. Nor do you worship (the Lord) Whom I worship. I shall never (ever) worship those (idols) that you worship. Nor shall you (ever) worship (the Lord) Whom I worship. (So) you have your Din (Religion) and I have my Dīn (Religion).'"[108]

This Constitution further substantiates this point in article thirty stating:

«وَإِنَّ يَهُودَ بَنِي عَوْفٍ أُمَّةٌ مَعَ الْمُؤْمِنِينَ لِلْيَهُودِ دِينُهُمْ وَلِلْمُسْلِمِينَ دِينُهُمْ».

"The Jews of Banū 'Awf (non-Muslim minorities) shall be considered a community alongside the believers. They shall be guaranteed the rights of religious freedom along with the Muslims."[109]

From article thirty to forty the Holy Prophet (blessings and peace be upon him) mentioned each and every Jewish tribe specifically

108 Al-Qur'ān, al-Kāfirūn, 109: 1-6.

109 Related by Ibn Hishām in *al-Sīra al-Nabawiyya*, vol. 3, p. 34; Abū 'Ubayd al-Qāsim in *Kitāb al-Amwāl*, vol. 1, p. 263; Ibn Zanjuway in *Kitāb al-Amwāl*, p. 392; Ibn Taymiyya in *al-Ṣārim al-Maslūl*, p. 63; Ibn al-Qayyim in *Aḥkām Ahl al-Dhimma*, vol. 3, p. 1407; Ibn Kathīr in *al-Bidāya wa al-Nihāya*, vol. 2, p. 261; Ibn Sayyid al-Nās, vol. 1, p. 228; al-Suhaylī in *al-Rawḍ al-Unuf*, vol. 2, p. 349; and al-Ṣāliḥī in *Subul al-Hudā wa al-Rishād*, vol. 3, p. 382.

by name, guaranteeing them their right of protection under the new Constitution.

The Qur'ān also states:

﴿لَآ إِكۡرَاهَ فِي ٱلدِّينِۖ﴾.

"There is no compulsion in Dīn (Religion)."[110]

There can be no narrowness in Islām, nor can there be any inconvenience. A Muslim cannot enforce hardship on another person or compel others to their way: forced conversions have no place in this pure religion. Compelling others to embrace Islām is against Islām and the teachings of the Qur'ān. Everybody has a right to practice his/her own religion; rather Islām has enjoined Muslim rulers to protect the places of worship of non-Muslims.

In the days of Banū Umayya (Omayyad Dynasty), Walīd b. 'Abd al-Malik, one of the Umayyad governors, demolished a portion of a church in Damascus, and had extended a mosque in its stead. When the caliph 'Umar b. 'Abd al-'Azīz (may Allāh be well pleased with him) got the news, he ordered that the extended portion of the mosque be demolished and the church should be rebuilt, and it was done. The tradition says:

فَلَمَّا اسْتَخْلَفَ عُمَرُ بْنُ عَبْدِ الْعَزِيْزِ رضي الله عنه، شَكَى النَّصَارَى إِلَيْهِ مَا فَعَلَ الْوَلِيْدُ بِهِمْ فِي كَنِيْسَتِهِمْ، فَكَتَبَ إِلَى عَامِلِهِ يَأْمُرُهُ بِرَدِّ مَا زَادَهُ فِي الْمَسْجِدِ.

[110] Al-Qur'ān, *al-Baqara*, 2: 256.

"When 'Umar b. 'Abd al-'Azīz (may Allāh be well pleased with him) took over as Caliph, the Christians complained to him about al-Walīd's forcible occupation of Church land. He ordered the official to get that part of the Mosque demolished, which had been constructed on the land of Church, and return it to Christians. So the same was done."[111]

Freedom of expression; the rights of ill people and elderly citizens, the right of protection for one's property, and the right of forming contracts were all guaranteed under the new Constitution.

5.3 FORBIDDANCE OF BLOODSHED

The Constitution forbade fighting and bloodshed amongst the various communities of the state:

«وَإِنَّ يَثْرِبَ حَرَامٌ جَوْفُهَا لِأَهْلِ هَذِهِ الصَّحِيفَةِ».

"The valley of Yathrib is sacred and there shall be prohibition of fighting and bloodshed among the various communities of the state."[112]

Likewise, as stated in article sixty-one, any oppressor, militant, or tyrant that commits an act of cruelty, oppression or suppression is to be deprived of the protection given by the Constitution:

«وَإِنَّهُ لَا يَحُولُ هَذَا الْكِتَابُ دُونَ ظَالِمٍ وَآثِمٍ».

"This constitutional document shall not protect any traitor or oppressor."[113]

---

111 Related by al-Balādhurī in *Futūḥ al-Buldān*, p. 150.

112 Related by Ibn Hishām in *al-Sīra al-Nabawiyya*, vol. 3, p. 34; Abū 'Ubayd al-Qāsim in *Kitāb al-Amwāl*, vol. 1, p. 263; and Ibn Zanjuway in *Kitāb al-Amwāl*, p. 206.

113 Related by Ibn Hishām in *al-Sīra al-Nabawiyya*, vol. 3, p. 35; Abū 'Ubayd al-Qāsim in *Kitāb al-Amwāl*, vol. 1, p. 263; Ibn Zanjuway in *Kitāb al-Amwāl*, p. 206; Ibn Sayyid al-Nās, vol. 1, p. 228; al-Suhaylī in *al-Rawḍ al-Unuf*, vol. 2, p. 350; and al-Ṣāliḥī in *Subul al-Hudā wa al-Rishād*, vol. 3, p. 383.

Furthermore, in the penultimate article - sixty-two, the Constitution states:

«وَإِنَّهُ مَنْ خَرَجَ آمِنٌ وَمَنْ قَعَدَ آمِنٌ بِالْمَدِينَةِ إِلَّا مَنْ ظَلَمَ أَوْ أَثِمَ».

"Whoever goes out (on a military expedition) shall be provided with security and whoever stays in Medina shall have likewise, except those who commit oppression and violate the content of this Constitution."[114]

Ultimately, the Constitution guaranteed protection to peaceful citizens, whilst those people who worked against the peace and security of the state and its people, would lose their guaranteed Constitutional protection for their life.

The final article sixty-three, states:

«وَإِنَّ اللهَ جَارٌ لِمَنْ بَرَّ وَاتَّقَى وَمُحَمَّدٌ رَسُولُ اللهِ».

"Allāh and the Prophet, the Messenger of God, are the protectors of good citizens and of those who fear Allāh."[115]

5.4 PROTECTION OF HUMAN LIFE

Many of the fundamental human rights which we enjoy today were declared by the Holy Prophet (blessings and peace be upon

---

[114] Related by Ibn Hishām in *al-Sīra al-Nabawiyya*, vol. 3, p. 35; Abū 'Ubayd al-Qāsim in *Kitāb al-Amwāl*, vol. 1, p. 263; Ibn Zanjuway in *Kitāb al-Amwāl*, p. 206; Ibn Sayyid al-Nās, vol. 1, p. 229; al-Suhaylī in *al-Rawḍ al-Unuf*, vol. 2, p. 350; Ibn Kathīr in *al-Bidāya wa al-Nihāya*, vol. 2, p. 262; and al-Ṣāliḥī in *Subul al-Hudā wa al-Rishād*, vol. 3, p. 383.

[115] Related by Ibn Hishām in *al-Sīra al-Nabawiyya*, vol. 3, p. 35; Ibn Zanjuway in *Kitāb al-Amwāl*, p. 206; al-Suhaylī in *al-Rawḍ al-Unuf*, vol. 2, p. 350; and Ibn Kathīr in *al-Bidāya wa al-Nihāya*, vol. 2, p. 226.

him) through the Holy Qur'ān and his practice. The right to the protection of life was declared in chapter five of the Holy Qur'ān, verse thirty-two, in which Allāh states:

﴿مَن قَتَلَ نَفْسًا بِغَيْرِ نَفْسٍ أَوْ فَسَادٍ فِي ٱلْأَرْضِ فَكَأَنَّمَا قَتَلَ ٱلنَّاسَ جَمِيعًا وَمَنْ أَحْيَاهَا فَكَأَنَّمَآ أَحْيَا ٱلنَّاسَ جَمِيعًا﴾.

"whoever killed a person (unjustly), except as a punishment for murder or for (spreading) disorder in the land, it would be as if he killed all the people (of society); and whoever (saved him from unjust murder and) made him survive, it would be as if he saved the lives of all the people (of society; i.e. he rescued the collective system of human life)."[116]

Therefore, the murder of any human being regardless of their religion, race or colour is forbidden in Islām and doing so amounts to the murder of humanity. Similarly, serving one person is equivalent to serving the whole of mankind.

In fact, those who are in the womb of their mothers have also been guaranteed this right to life; because the right to life is such a precious thing that nobody can act against the life of any person.

Mankind has been accorded with such respect and honour that even after his death, no one is permitted to abuse the deceased body, whether he or she is a Muslim or non Muslim. Narrated by 'Ā'isha (may Allāh be well pleased with her):

قَالَ النَّبِيُّ ﷺ: «لَا تَسُبُّوا الْأَمْوَاتَ فَإِنَّهُمْ قَدْ أَفْضَوْا إِلَى مَا قَدَّمُوا».

116 Al-Qur'ān, *al-Mā'ida*, 5: 32.

"The Prophet (blessing and peace be upon him) said, 'Do not abuse the dead ones, because they have reached the result of what they forwarded.'"[117]

It is narrated in an agreed upon tradition:

عَنْ جَابِرِ بْنِ عَبْدِ اللهِ رضي الله عنهما، قَالَ: مَرَّ بِنَا جَنَازَةٌ فَقَامَ لَهَا النَّبِيُّ صلى الله عليه وآله وسلم، وَقُمْنَا بِهِ، فَقُلْنَا: يَا رَسُولَ اللهِ! إِنَّهَا جَنَازَةُ يَهُودِيٍّ. قَالَ صلى الله عليه وآله وسلم: «إِذَا رَأَيْتُمُ الْجَنَازَةَ فَقُومُوا».

"Jābir b. 'Abd Allāh (may Allāh be well pleased with him) narrates: 'A funeral passed us by and the Prophet (blessings and peace be upon him) stood up for it. We stood up, and then we said: O Messenger of Allāh, it is a funeral of a Jew. The Prophet (blessings and peace be upon him) replied: If you see a funeral stand.'"[118]

Notice, when the Companions (may Allāh be well pleased with them) enquired about the Prophet's action and had informed him that the funeral passing by him was not that of a Muslim but a Jew; the Prophet (may Allāh be well pleased with them) showed no concern for the religion or the culture of that person. Instead, he expressed his respect stating that the funerals of all people are to

---

117 Related by al-Bukhārī in *al-Ṣaḥīḥ*, vol. 1, p. 470 # 1329; al-Nasā'ī in *al-Sunan*, vol. 4, p. 53 # 1936; and *al-Sunan al-Kubrā*, vol. 1, p. 630 # 2063; Ibn Ḥibbān in *al-Ṣaḥīḥ*, vol. 7, p. 291 # 3021; Aḥmad b. Ḥanbal in *al-Musnad*, vol. 6, p. 180 # 25509; al-Dārimī in *al-Sunan*, vol. 2, p. 311 # 2511; al-Ḥākim in *al-Mustadrak*, vol. 1, p. 541 # 419; and al-Bayhaqī in *al-Sunan al-Kubrā*, vol. 4, p. 75 # 6979; and *Shu'ab al-Īmān*, vol. 5, p. 287 # 6678.

118 Related by al-Bukhārī in *al-Ṣaḥīḥ*, vol. 1, p. 441 # 1249; Muslim in *al-Ṣaḥīḥ*, vol. 2, p. 660 # 960; al-Nasā'ī in *al-Sunan*, vol. 4, p. 45 # 1922; and *al-Sunan al-Kubrā*, vol. 1, p. 626 # 2049; and Aḥmad b. Ḥanbal in *al-Musnad*, vol. 3, p. 319 # 14467.

be respected, as this is a fundamental human right that transcends all divides.

Islām has accorded respect and honour to every man and woman in that nobody is allowed to insult or curse another. The Holy Prophet (blessings and peace be upon him) has even prohibited the Muslims from cursing or torturing animals and insects.

'Abd al-Raḥmān b. 'Abd Allāh quoted his father as saying that once they were on a journey in the company of Allāh's Messenger (blessings and peace be upon him) and he had gone to relieve himself. The Companions (may Allāh be well pleased with them) saw a sparrow with two young ones. When they took the young ones, the sparrow, greatly upset, came and began to spread out its wings. When the Holy Prophet (blessings and peace be upon him) returned, he said:

«مَنْ فَجَعَ هَذِهِ بِوَلَدِهَا؟ رُدُّوا وَلَدَهَا إِلَيْهَا».

"Who has pained this one by the (loss of) her young ones? Give her young ones back to her."[119]

Then the Holy Prophet (blessings and peace be upon him) saw an anthill, which had been burned. He declared such an act prohibited:

«إِنَّهُ لَا يَنْبَغِي أَنْ يُعَذِّبَ بِالنَّارِ إِلَّا رَبُّ النَّارِ».

"It is not fitting that anyone should punish with fire but the Lord of the fire."[120]

---

119 Related by Abū Dāwūd in *al-Sunan*, vol. 3, p. 55 # 2675.

120 Related by Abū Dāwūd in *al-Sunan*, vol. 3, p. 55 # 2675.

'Abd Allāh b. 'Umar (may Allāh be well pleased with him) narrated that Allāh's Messenger (blessings and peace be upon him) stated:

«عُذِّبَتِ امْرَأَةٌ فِي هِرَّةٍ حَبَسَتْهَا، حَتَّى مَاتَتْ
جُوعًا، فَدَخَلَتْ فِيهَا النَّارَ». قَالَ: «فَقَالَ: وَاللهُ
أَعْلَمُ، لَا أَنْتِ أَطْعَمْتِهَا وَلَا سَقَيْتِهَا حِينَ
حَبَسْتِيهَا، وَلَا أَنْتِ أَرْسَلْتِهَا فَأَكَلَتْ مِنْ خَشَاشِ
الْأَرْضِ».

"A woman was tortured and was put in Hell because of a cat which she had kept locked till it died of hunger. Allāh's Messenger (blessings and peace be upon him) further said, Allāh knows better. Allah said (to the woman), 'You neither fed it nor watered when you locked it up, nor did you set it free to eat the insects of the earth.'"[121]

5.5 RIGHT OF PRIVACY

Likewise, Islām has given man the right of privacy. Allāh (SWT) states:

﴿يَٰٓأَيُّهَا ٱلَّذِينَ ءَامَنُواْ لَا تَدۡخُلُواْ بُيُوتًا غَيۡرَ
بُيُوتِكُمۡ حَتَّىٰ تَسۡتَأۡنِسُواْ وَتُسَلِّمُواْ عَلَىٰٓ

121 Related by al-Bukhārī in *al-□a□ī□*, vol. 2, p. 834 # 2236; Muslim in *al-□a□ī□*, vol. 4, p. 1760 # 2242; al-Dārimī in *al-Sunan*, vol. 2, p. 426 # 2814; and al-Bayhaqī in *al-Sunan al-Kubrā*, vol. 5, p. 214 # 9851.

أَهْلِهَا ۚ ذَٰلِكُمْ خَيْرٌ لَّكُمْ لَعَلَّكُمْ تَذَكَّرُونَ ﴿٢٧﴾.

"O believers! Do not enter houses other than your own until you obtain their permission. And greet their residents (immediately after you enter). This (advice) is better for you so that you may contemplate (its rationale)."[122]

5.6 RIGHT OF EQUALITY

Furthermore, the right of security was also guaranteed by the Holy Prophet (blessings and peace be upon him), as well as human equality. Human equality was guaranteed by ensuring legal, social and economic equality (as far as the basic needs are concerned in the form of social and income support). The Holy Prophet (blessings and peace be upon him) declared:

«لَا فَضْلَ لِعَرَبِيٍّ عَلَى أَعْجَمِيٍّ، وَلَا لِعَجَمِيٍّ عَلَى عَرَبِيٍّ، وَلَا لِأَحْمَرَ عَلَى أَسْوَدَ، وَلَا أَسْوَدَ عَلَى أَحْمَرَ إِلَّا بِالتَّقْوَى».

"No Arab is superior to a non-Arab, and no non-Arab is superior to an Arab; no red person has a superiority over a black person, and no black person has superiority over a red person, except for those who are God-fearing."[123]

That is to say that superiority is based only on the character and moral integrity of a person, not on one's race, religion, or colour.

---

[122] Al-Qur'ān, *al-Nūr*, 24: 27.

[123] Related by Aḥmad b. Ḥanbal in *al-Musnad*, vol. 5, p. 411; Ibn al-Mubārak in *al-Musnad*, p. 147 # 239; and Haythamī in *Majma' al-Zawā'id*, vol. 3, p. 266.

5.7 GUARANTEE OF LEGAL JUSTICE

Another constitutional guarantee provided by Islām through the Holy Qur'ān and through the Holy Prophet (blessings and peace be upon him), was the guarantee of legal justice.

The Qur'ān states;

﴿وَإِذَا حَكَمْتُم بَيْنَ ٱلنَّاسِ أَن تَحْكُمُوا۟ بِٱلْعَدْلِ﴾.

"And when you judge matters among people, give judgment with justice."[124]

This guarantee of legal equality and justice is an absolute statement of the Qur'ān and there is no mentioning of faith or religion. Thus, it is a universal right for the whole of mankind. Likewise, it is stated:

﴿إِنَّ ٱللَّهَ يَأْمُرُكُمْ أَن تُؤَدُّوا۟ ٱلْأَمَـٰنَـٰتِ إِلَىٰٓ أَهْلِهَا﴾.

"Surely, Allāh commands you to entrust the belongings to those who are worthy of them."[125]

This is a general commandment that states whenever you are appointed or given an authority to adjudicate a matter, you are required to administer justice fairly regardless of the person's religion.

---

[124] Al-Qur'ān, *al-Nisā'*, 4: 58.

[125] Al-Qur'ān, *al-Nisā'*, 4: 58.

The Qur'ān states:

﴿يَـٰٓأَيُّهَا ٱلَّذِينَ ءَامَنُوا۟ كُونُوا۟ قَوَّٰمِينَ بِٱلْقِسْطِ
شُهَدَآءَ لِلَّهِ وَلَوْ عَلَىٰٓ أَنفُسِكُمْ أَوِ ٱلْوَٰلِدَيْنِ
وَٱلْأَقْرَبِينَ ۚ إِن يَكُنْ غَنِيًّا أَوْ فَقِيرًا فَٱللَّهُ أَوْلَىٰ
بِهِمَا ۖ﴾.

> *"O believers! Become tenaciously firm on justice, bearing witness (merely) for the sake of Allāh even if (the witness) is against your own selves or (your) parents or (your) relatives. Whether the person (against whom is the evidence) is rich or poor, Allāh is a greater Well-Wisher of them both (than you are)."*[126]

That is to say that one has to administer justice on this earth and to become a witness to Almighty Allāh.

5.8 GUARANTEE OF FREE-TRIAL

The guarantee of a hearing and a free-trial was given to every person and nobody would be punished without a proper, independent hearing, this also included the right of defence. Furthermore, freedom and liberty were also guaranteed; these concepts of human liberty and freedom were implemented many centuries later in other civilizations but these were promulgated, practiced, and enforced by Islām in the 7th Century.

5.9 DEFENCE OF THE STATE OF MEDINA

Interestingly, if one was to observe the first ten years of the Holy Prophet's life in Medina as head of the state up to the point of the

---

126 Al-Qur'ān, *al-Nisā'*, 4: 135.

conquest of Makkah, one would note that no war was fought on the borders of Makkah. All wars were imposed on the society of Medina and were fought on the borders of Medina, or within close proximity of the city-state. The first major battle was Badr in which there was an advancement and aggression by the Makkans. The second major battle was Uḥud which was fought at a distance of two miles away from Medina. Another major battle was the 'Battle of the Trench' which was fought on the very borders of Medina, when a trench was prepared to defend the city-state. Within those years there was no advancement or war of aggression by the Holy Prophet (blessings and peace be upon him) until after the Treaty of Ḥudaybiya, when a ten year no-war pact was made with the Makkans in the 6th year of Hegira. However, after a year, the Makkans broke the contract. So the Prophet (blessings and peace be upon him) made an advancement to conquer Makkah, which he did without shedding a single drop of blood.

When the Muslims had entered the city as conquerors, one of the Companions, Ansarite commander Sa'd b. 'Ibāda (may Allāh be well pleased with him) declared vehemently, 'today is the day of revenge.' For almost two decades, the Muslims had suffered under the hands of the Makkans and were forced to abandon their homes. So, the desire to exact revenge on their former oppressors was a natural reaction on that historic occasion. Emotions were running high, but when the Holy Prophet (blessings and peace be upon him) heard his Companion's calling for retribution, he stood up and addressed the whole of Makkah and said:

«اَلْيَوْمُ يَوْمُ الْمَرْحَمَةِ».

"(No! Today is not the day of revenge:) Today is the day of mercy and forgiveness."[127]

The Holy Prophet (blessings and peace be upon him) forgave and pardoned his enemies and set a precedent that was to be the distinctive hallmark of Islām from then on. The Holy Prophet (blessings and peace be upon him) said:

«مَنْ دَخَلَ دَارَ أَبِي سُفْيَانَ فَهُوَ آمِنٌ، وَمَنْ أَلْقَى السِّلَاحَ فَهُوَ آمِنٌ، وَمَنْ أَغْلَقَ بَابَهُ فَهُوَ آمِنٌ».

"Whoever enters Abū Sufyān's house will attain security and whoever lays aside his arms will attain security and whoever shuts his gate will attain security."[128]

Unfortunately, and it is a matter of great shame that some criminals in our time have brought about a bad name to Islām through their own criminal activities and out of their own political agenda. Whilst at the same time the mistakes have been committed from the other side too, through their actions and foreign policies. There is a great misunderstanding between the West and Islām. If the true face of Islām is identified and its true teachings properly understood, then much progress would be made towards the restoration of world peace, as well as reconciliation and co-operation between the two civilizations. Terrorists have no religion, nor do they have any attachment to culture; they have no faith and are enemies of humanity, as well as the enemies of Islām.

---

127 Related by Ibn Ḥajar al-'Asqalānī in *Fatḥ al-Bārī*, vol. 8, pp. 8, 9; and Ibn 'Abd al-Barr in *al-Istī' āb*, vol. 2, p. 163.

128 Related by Muslim in *al-Ṣaḥīḥ*, vol. 3, p. 1407 # 1780; Abū Dāwūd in *al-Sunan*, vol. 3, p. 162 # 3021; and al-Bazzār in *al-Musnad*, vol. 4, p. 122 # 1292.

- PART 3B -
AL-HIDAYAH EUROPE 2009: QUESTION & ANSWER SESSION (U.K)

Q1. REGARDING WHETHER TERRORISM IS CAUSED BY FACTORS WITHIN ISLĀM OR OUTSIDE ISLĀM

Dr. Tahir Abbas (Director of the Centre for the Study of Ethnicity and Culture, University of Birmingham): Shaykh-ul-Islām, thank you for that very significant presentation. I'd like to draw your attention to the issues of the contemporary period. You highlighted towards the end that how those who allude to terrorism and use the name of Islām are criminals, they have subverted classical teachings. I'd like you to elaborate on when you think that began to go wrong: is it a function of internal problems or are the external policy dilemmas more of an issue? Please can you elaborate?

Shaykh-ul-Islām Dr Muhammad Tahir-ul-Qadri: This is a very interesting question to which I would like to give a brief answer. In my opinion this is not just an internal matter. This kind of terrorism has emerged out of an international political agenda. I was born in Pakistan, I spent my whole life there, and there were no acts of terrorism in Pakistan 20-25 years before: there were Muslims, there were religious institutions, and there were mosques, but we never came across any suicidal bombings, or any acts of terrorism. This developed when a sponsored war was fought against the illegal occupation of Afghanistan by Russia. At that time a global power wanted to fight against a Russian occupation and so certain people from the Arab world and in Afghanistan were sponsored: they were provided with arms and ammunition, money and training. That was the time when Osama Bin Laden became one of the heroes and that was the time when the Taliban came into existence.

This sponsored war against Russian occupation was fought, forcing the Russians to leave the land of Afghanistan. Then the sponsors left these terrorists to their own devices. They were then utilized to carry out their terroristic activities in Kashmir. When they were banned from fighting in Kashmir, they started to spread in Pakistan and they had nothing to do except killing, because this was the skill which they were taught. So I think a political global agenda was the basis for the emergence of terrorism: these terrorists in Pakistan have advanced arms and logistics which even the Pakistani army does not possess, as well as money (to carry out their activities). The question is where do they get all of this from? How did Baitullah Mehsud become a giant from just an ordinary person? How did the Taliban become giants from just ordinary students of *madrasas*?

To eliminate them we have to decide whether elimination of terrorism is our humanistic agenda or our expansionistic agenda. I think, sincerely and honestly, if eradication and elimination of terrorism from the whole world is our humanistic agenda, then elimination of terrorism is not a matter of 1 to 2 years, but if it is a political and expansionistic agenda then it will continue for the whole century.

Q2. REGARDING THE PROSPECT OF MUSLIMS SUPPORTING TERRORISM

Phil Rees (prominent journalist and producer): Hello Shaykh-ul-Islām, thank you for inviting me here. I covered the war in Afghanistan in the 1980s and later of course the war in Bosnia and in both cases, Muslims felt a duty to help their brothers and sisters in distress. I think everyone here will know the Hadith of course, of the 'one body' when one part of the body is ill the whole body feels ill. At that time, I remember coming up to Coventry, people were raising money for people in Bosnia who were suffering and it would seem as a very proud thing to do, a proper thing to do; obviously to do that now would be considered an act of terrorism where there are foreign armies occupying *Dār al-Islām*, or at least have their presence there. How would you see the two and compare the two in terms of duty of Muslims to help their brothers?

Shaykh-ul-Islām Dr Muḥammad Tahir-ul-Qadri: Thank you, I understand and agree with you that the whole of the Muslim Umma is like a body, but remember there are different organs to that body. Working as a body, no doubt that it is required in Islām and it has been practiced in the past, but at the same time if a single organ of that body becomes cancerous then the other organs are not supposed to support that cancer, instead they will support the surgeon to cut this cancerous organ off! Because by doing so the whole body will be protected from the spreading of that cancer.

Terrorism is no less than a cancer: if any part of the Muslim world or any group begins terrorist activities, it means that there is a cancer in this body of Muslims. So, the Muslims are compulsorily required to help the surgeon to remove that part of the body so that the remaining portion of the body is safe. That is why terrorist activities can never be supported by any Muslim, even if the terrorists abuse the name of *jihād*.

Jihād is never an act of terrorism: *jihād* is to fight against terrorism. The concept of *jihād* is a struggle, a sacred struggle, against the evil desires of our lower self. *Jihād* is a sacred struggle to spread knowledge and to remove ignorance within society. *Jihād* is a sacred struggle for charity, to remove any economic unbalance and to fight against poverty and to bring about its elimination. *Jihād* is a sacred struggle to free and liberate people from acts of oppression like the injustices of Saddam or the Taliban who have given a really bad name to Islām. The Muslims as a body should never support a cancerous organ. We have to differentiate between what is right and what is wrong.

Q3. REGARDING THE MISUSE OF THE BLASPHEMY LAW AGAINST PAKISTANI CHRISTIANS

Canon Dr Christopher Lamb (representative of Archbishop of Canterbury Dr Rowan Williams): Shaykh... I would like to echo the thanks of others to the invitation.

Shaykh-ul-Islām Dr Muḥammad Tahir-ul-Qadri: You're welcome. You know many Christian scholars and bishops in Pakistan, such as Dr Andrew Francis and Dr Azaria who are the representatives of the Catholic Church; I always invite them, and we celebrate Christmas every year at our (Central) Secretariat, (Lahore); and we always open our mosque for our Christian brothers to worship according to their faith - this is our practice. So you should feel at home; you are not our guest, you may consider yourself as the host of this session!

Canon Dr Christopher Lamb: Shukriya (thank-you), I do indeed feel at home and you mentioned the Christians of Pakistan, it's them who I have in mind. I'm thankful for your words about freedom of religion in Islām and freedom to believe and not to be compelled otherwise. There is, however, a problem in Pakistan which you will be familiar with, in the operation of the blasphemy law which on a number of occasions very recently has caused considerable trouble for Christians when false allegations have been made that the Qur'ān has been defaced or spoiled in some way. Only 10 days ago, 30 Christian homes were destroyed and people killed and the fire fighters were prevented from going to help those people. It must also be said that there were Muslims who helped the Christians in that situation, but I wanted to ask you about the operation of the blasphemy law which has been misused and exploited both against Christians and also against fellow Muslims, and I wonder really about the wisdom of it.

Shaykh-ul-Islām Dr Muḥammad Tahir-ul-Qadri: Thank you, I agree with your concern, I absolutely agree with your concern, but let me explain. You know the law is of two kinds: one is the substantive aspect of law and the other is the procedural and adjective aspect of law. When we talk of the law of blasphemy; there is nothing wrong as far as the substantive aspect of the law is concerned. I as a student of Law, having been a professor of Law throughout my career - I can say that there is nothing wrong with regards to the substantive aspect of the law. When you use the word 'misuse' it makes the case clear. The wrong which we see is in the adjective and procedural aspect of the law. This is not a law against the Christian community, this is a matter of corruption in the police force.

The problem is that the corrupt police officers are used to taking bribes. They don't just register cases wrongly against Christians, they register cases against poor Muslims too, either under the pressure of the landlords, or under the pressure of the MNA's ("members of national and provincial assemblies") and other influential political figures. They register the case of theft against people. This is a misuse of the law of theft; they register the case of fornication against people - this is a misuse of the law of adultery; there are hundreds and thousands of cases being registered in police stations everyday against poor and weak people. So every law is being misused whether in its original sense it was correct or wrong, every single law is being misused. Even the constitution is being misused by military dictators and they take over the charge. The influential people always misuse the laws, because there is no proper administration of justice, and the people working as police officers are not like those who are the police officers of British society and the Western world. There is a hell of a difference between the Pakistani police officer and the British police officer. So, the basic thing is to stop the misuse of law because there is no problem with the law itself. Some amendments according to me are necessarily required in procedural law.

I support that every police officer in the police station should not be allowed to register a case against any non-Muslim. The authority to trial any law of blasphemy should be given to a single magistrate in the district and after full scrutiny the case should go on trial; no police officer should be authorised to trial or investigate the cases. Only the men of integrity should be authorised to trial the case, so that they are also safe and the same kind of administration of justice should be applied to poor members of Pakistani society. This is a matter of corruption, not a matter of religion.

Q4. REGARDING ADVICE TO WESTERN GOVERNMENTS

Maqsood Ahmed (Senior Advisor from Communities Ministry): As-Salām-u 'Alaykum Qibla Ḥuzūr, Shaykh-ul-Islām. I have been listening to you this morning and this afternoon as well. I think what I hear from yourself and from the hall is the voice of reason and moderation, but our difficulty in the British community and the British Muslim community is that we don't have many voices of reason. Looking at your eminent colleague Dr Safarāz Na'īmī (and his martyrdom) who gave that same voice of reason as you are giving; those voices are silenced by the terrorists. How could you advise us to help to raise the voice of reason? *Jazāk Allāh Khayr.*

Shaykh-ul-Islām Dr Muḥammad Tahir-ul-Qadri: My brief advice on this subject is that I would like to ask the global authorities and the global powers, please, please, and please, don't help the friends of terrorists, just help the friends of peace.

I know in Pakistan as well as in the other parts of the world, there are people who are very clever and who work very closely with the British and Western European governments, but they may have some close relationship with those parties and groups who have extreme ideas, and those groups who have very extreme ideas are closely linked with the terrorists, and they are known to be the friends and reliable persons and colleagues of the Western and British governments. So, you have to discriminate between friends and enemies. This is my only advice.

I think up till now the Western world has not been able to discriminate between their real friends and their real enemies. The day when they will discriminate between their real friends and their real enemies in connection to the war against terrorism, *in shā Allāh*, the war against terrorism will definitively reach the stage of success.

Q5. REGARDING A RESEARCH PATH TO FOLLOW FOR PROMOTING THE POSITIVE CO-EXISTENCE OF MUSLIMS IN UK SOCIETY

Dr Sophie Gilliat-Ray, Director, Centre for the Study of Islām in the UK, Cardiff University: Thank you very much indeed for this opportunity to address a question to you. In the research centre that I direct at Cardiff University, our underlining mission is the promotion of understanding of Islām and the life of Muslims in Britain. And we work in a very close partnership with the local Muslim community and the Muslim council of Wales in trying to fulfil that ambition. I'm not an Islāmic scholar but I am academic and I would really like your advice based on your engagement with British Muslims and your understanding of the situation in relation to Islām in Britain. What do you think is the most important priority for a research centre such as mine at Cardiff University?

Shaykh-ul-Islām Dr Muḥammad Tahir-ul-Qadri: Thank you, I think the most effective and influential role to be played by the research centre is to promote the real and correct concept of integration. There are three models that a minority can adopt within a larger society such as Britain. These three models are the model of isolation, the model of annihilation/assimilation, and the model of integration.

There are some Muslims who consider themselves to be practicing and devout, but love to remain in the model of isolation. You have to produce research in order to develop their understanding that living in isolation and not interacting with the wider community is totally against the teachings of Islām, as well as going against the general ethos of being a member of society; it is important that they understand that being part and parcel of British society is absolutely in accordance with the teachings of Islām. So, they have to come out, and you have to help to bring them out of isolation. This would be the message for the religious people and Muslims in general.

And, on the other hand, you have to promote research for the British government stating that bringing them out from isolation does not mean that they have to adopt the model of annihilation or assimilation. The research should try to address the issue that the model of isolation will be damaging for the Muslims, whilst on the other hand, the model of annihilation will be damaging for British society. Annihilation is never a good model because every culture has its own roots and identity; and every culture has its own traits and attributes. So, when you take them out from isolation, you have to ensure at the same time that you protect them from the annihilation model, because this will create a reaction. So, your research should follow these lines.

The best future for British society is indeed the model of integration. What does it mean? Integration is the full and active participation of minorities within society with a guaranteed protection of their cultural identity, as well as their religious identity. If this path is adopted then this will lead to a multicultural society, and then finally this multiculturalism itself will become a culture! So your research; and your seminars, and your printed material should aim to give a message to both sides: one to the Muslims arguing the case that you have to come out of isolation and become part and parcel of British society; and on the other hand a message should go to the governments to warn them of the pitfalls in the model of annihilation or assimilation, by telling policy makers and politicians alike that they should not advance policies that subdue the identity of minorities. This will hopefully lead to the development of integration. If this model of integration is carried out successfully then British society will indeed be one of the most prosperous societies. I do believe that the British society is one of the best societies of the Western world! - it is a multicultural society. Since I am a Canadian citizen, I would say that my Canadian society is in fact the best in the world, but at the same time I can see that Britain is also working on the same lines. So the protection of the splendour and diversity of British society, and its value, lies in multiculturalism; and multiculturalism can only be protected through integration. This is the work that needs to be done. Thank You.

BIBLIOGRAPHY

1. al-Qur'ān.

ḤĀDĪTH

1. 'Abd al-Razzāq, Abū Bakr b. al-Hammām b. al-Nāfi' al-Ṣan'ānī (126-211/744-826), *al-Muṣannaf,* Beirut, Lebanon: al-Maktab al-Islāmī, 1403 AH.
2. Aḥmad b. Ḥanbal, Abū 'Abd Allāh b. Muḥammad (164-241/780-855), *al-Musnad,* Beirut, Lebanon: al-Maktab al-Islāmī, 1398/1978.
3. al-Bayhaqī, Abū Bakr Aḥmad b. al-Ḥusayn (384-458/994-1066), *Shu'ab al-Īmān,* Beirut, Lebanon: Dār al-Kutub al-'Ilmiyya, 1410/1990.
4. al-Bayhaqī, Abū Bakr Aḥmad b. al-Ḥusayn (384-458/994-1066), *as-Sunan al-Kubrā,* Makka, Saudi Arabia: Maktaba Dār al-Bāz, 1414/1994.
5. al-Bazzār, Abū Bakr Aḥmad b. 'Amr b. 'Abd al-Khāliq al-Baṣrī (210-292/825-905), *al-Musnad,* Beirut, Lebanon: Mu'assisa 'Ulūm al-Qur'ān, 1409 AH.
6. al-Bukhārī, Abū 'Abd Allāh Muḥammad b. Ismā'īl b. Ibrāhīm (194-256/810-870), *al-Ṣaḥīḥ*, Beirut, Lebanon: Dār Ibn Kathīr, al-Yamāma, 1407/1987.
7. al-Bukhārī, Abū 'Abd Allāh Muḥammad b. Ismā'īl b. Ibrāhīm (194-256/810-870), *al-Adab al-Mufrad,* Damascus, Syria: Dār al-Qalam, 1st ed. 1422/2001.
8. al-Dāraquṭnī, Abū al-Ḥasan 'Alī b. 'Umar (306-385/918-995), *al-Sunan*, Beirut, Lebanon: 'Ālim al-Kutub, 4th ed. 1406/1986.
9. al-Dāraquṭnī, Abū al-Ḥasan 'Alī b. 'Umar (306-385/918-995), *al-Sunan*, Beirut, Lebanon: Dār al-Ma'rifa, 1386/1966.

10. al-Dārimī, Abū Muḥammad ʻAbd Allāh (181-255/797-869), *al-Sunan*, Beirut, Lebanon: Dār al-Kitāb al-ʻArabī, 1407 AH.
11. al-Daylamī, Abū Shujāʻ Shīrawayh b. Shardār b. Shīrawayh (445-509/1053-1115), *Musnad al-Firdaws*, Beirut, Lebanon: Dār al-Kutub al-ʻIlmiyya, 1406/1986.
12. Abū Dāwūd, Sulaymān b. Ashʻath (202-275/817-889), *al-Sunan*, Beirut, Lebanon: Dār al-Fikr, 1414/1994.
13. al-Ḥākim, Abū ʻAbd Allāh Muḥammad b. ʻAbd Allāh b. Muḥammad (321-405/933-1014), *al-Mustadrak ʻalā al-Ṣaḥīḥayn,* Beirut, Lebanon: Dār al-Kutub al-ʻIlmiyya, 1411/1990.
14. al-Haythamī, Nūr al-Dīn Abu al-Ḥasan ʻAlī b. Abī Bakr (735-807/1335-1405), *Majmaʻ al-Zawā'id,* Cairo, Egypt: Dār ar-Riyān li-t-Turāth & Beirut Lebanon: Dār al-Kitab al-ʻArabī, 1407/1987.
15. Ibn Ḥibbān, Abū Ḥātim Muḥammad b. Ḥibbān b. Aḥmad b. Ḥibbān (270-354/884-965), *al-Ṣaḥīḥ*, Beirut, Lebanon: Mu'assisa al-Risālah, 2nd ed. 1414/1993.
16. al-Hindī, ʻAlā al-Dīn ʻAlī al-Muttaqī b. Ḥassām al-Dīn (d. 975 AH), *Kanz al-ʻUmmāl fī Sunan al-Afʻāl wa al-Aqwāl*, Beirut, Lebanon: Mu'assisa al-Risāla, 2nd ed. 1399/1979.
17. Ibn Khuzayma, Abū Bakr Muḥammad b. Isḥāq (223-311/838-924), *al-Ṣaḥīḥ,* Beirut, Lebanon: al-Maktab al-Islāmī, 1390/1970.
18. al-Marwazī, Abū Bakr Aḥmad b. ʻAlī b. Saʻīd al-Umawī (d. 202-292 AH), *Musnad Abī Bakr al-Ṣiddīq,* Beirut, Lebanon: al-Maktab al-Islāmī.
19. Ibn Māja, Muḥammad b. Yazīd (209-273/824-887), *al-Sunan*, Beirut, Lebanon: Dār al-Kutub al-ʻIlmiyya, 1st ed. 1419/1998.
20. Ibn Māja, Muḥammad b. Yazīd (209-273/824-887), *al-Sunan*, Beirut, Lebanon: Dār al-Fikr.

21. Mālik, Ibn Anas b. Mālik b. Abī 'Āmir b. 'Amr b. al-Ḥārith al-Aṣbaḥī (93-179/712-795), *al-Muwaṭṭa'*, Beirut, Lebanon: Dār Iḥyā' at-Turāth al-'Arabī, 1406/1985.
22. Ibn Manda, Abū 'Abd Allāh Muḥammad b. Isḥāq (310-395/922-1005), *al-Īmān*, Beirut, Lebanon: Mu'assisa al-Risāla, 2nd ed. 1406 AH.
23. Ibn al-Mubārak, Abū 'Abd al-Raḥmān 'Abd Allāh b. Wāḍiḥ al-Marwazī (118-181/736-798), *Kitāb al-Zuhd*, Beirut, Lebanon: Dār al-Kutub al-'Ilmiyya.
24. Muslim, Ibn al-Ḥajjāj al-Qushayrī (206-261/821-875), *al-Ṣaḥīḥ*, Beirut, Lebanon: Dār Ihyā' al-Turāth al-'Arabī, n.d.
25. an-Nasā'ī, Aḥmad b. Shu'ayb Abū 'Abd al-Raḥmān (215-303/830-915), *al-Sunan,* Beirut, Lebanon: Dār al-Kutub al-'Ilmiyya, 1416/1995 & Ḥalb, Syria: Maktab al-Maṭbū'āt al-Islāmiyya, 1406/1986.
26. an-Nasā'ī, Aḥmad b. Shu'ayb Abū 'Abd al-Raḥmān (215-303/830-915), *al-Sunan al-Kubrā,* Beirut, Lebanon: Dār al-Kutub al-'Ilmiyya, 1411/1991.
27. Abū Nu'aym, Aḥmad b. 'Abd Allāh b. Aḥmad b. Isḥāq al-Aṣbahānī (336-430/948-1038), *Musnad al-Imām Abī Ḥanīfa,* Riyadh, Saudi Arabia, Maktabat al-Kawthar, 1415 AH.
28. al-Qaḍā'ī, Abū 'Abd Allāh Muḥammad b. Salama b. Ja'far b. 'Alī (d. 454/1062), *Musnad al-Shihāb*, Beirut, Lebanon: Mu'assisa al-Risāla, 1407 AH.
29. al-Shāfi'ī, Abū 'Abd Allāh Muḥammad b. Idrīs (150-204/767-819), *al-Musnad*, Beirut, Lebanon: Dār al-Kutub al-'Ilmiyya, 1st ed. 1400/1980.
30. al-Shāshī, Abū Sa'īd Haytham (d. 335/946 AH), *al-Musnad*, Medina, Saudi Arabia, Maktaba al-'Ulūm wa al-Ḥikam, 1410 AH.

31. Ibn Abī Shayba, Abū Bakr 'Abd Allāh b. Muḥammad b. Ibrāhīm (159-235/776-850), *al-Muṣannaf*, Riyadh, Saudi Arabia: Maktaba al-Rushd, 1409 AH.
32. al-Ṭabarānī, Sulaymān b. Aḥmad (260-360/873-971), *al-Mu'jam al-Awsaṭ*, Cairo, Egypt: Dār al-Ḥaramayn, 1415 AH.
33. al-Ṭabarānī, Sulaymān b. Aḥmad (260-360/873-971), *al-Mu'jam al-Kabīr*, Beirut, Lebanon: Dār Ihyā' al-Turāth al-'Arabī, n.d.
34. al-Ṭabarānī, Sulaymān b. Aḥmad (260-360/873-971), *al-Mu'jam al-Kabīr*, Mosul, Iraq: Maktaba al-'Ulūm wa al-Ḥikam, 1403/1983.
35. al-Tirmidhī, Abū 'Īsā Muḥammad b. 'Īsā (210-279/825-892), *al-Sunan*, Beirut, Lebanon: Dār al-Fikr, n.d.
36. al-Tirmidhī, Abū 'Īsā Muḥammad b. 'Īsā (210-279/825-892), *al-Sunan*, Beirut, Lebanon: Dār al-Iḥyā' at-Turāth.
37. Abū Ya'lā, Aḥmad b. 'Alī al-Mūṣilī al-Tamīmī (210-307/825-919), *al-Musnad*, Damascus, Syria: Dār al-Ma'mūn li-t-Turāth, 1404/1984.
38. al-Zayla'ī, Abū Muḥammad 'Abd Allāh b. Yūsuf al-Ḥanafī (d. 762/1360), *Naṣb al-Rāya li-Aḥadīth al-Hidāya*, Egypt: Dār al-Ḥadīth, 1357/1938.

TAFSĪR

39. al-Qurṭubī, Abū 'Abd Allāh Muḥammad b. Aḥmad b. Abī Bakr (d. 671 AH), *al-Jāmi' li-Aḥkām al-Qur'ān*, Cario, Egypt: Dār al-Shu'ab, 1372 AH.

ḤADĪTH COMMENTARIES

40. Ibn Ḥajar al-'Asqalānī, Aḥmad b. 'Alī b. Muḥammad b. Muḥammad b. 'Alī b. Aḥmad al-Kinānī (773-852/1372-1449), *Fatḥ al-Bārī Sharḥ Ṣaḥīḥ al-Bukarī*, Beirut, Lebanon, Dār al-Ma'rifa, 1379 AH.

41. Ibn Rajab al-Ḥanbalī, Abū al-Faraj 'Abd al-Raḥmān b. Aḥmad (736-795 AH), *Jāmi' al-'Ulūm wa al-Ḥikam fī Sharḥ Khamsīn Ḥadīth min Jawāmi' al-Kalim*, Beirut, Lebanon: Dār al-Ma'rifa, 1408 AH.

ASMĀ' AL-RIJĀL

42. Ibn 'Abd al-Barr, Abū 'Umar Yūsuf b. 'Abd Allāh b. Muḥammad (368-463/979-1071), *al-Istī'āb fī Ma'rifa al-Aṣḥāb*, Beirut, Lebanon: Dār al-Kutub al-'Ilmiyya, 2nd ed. 1422/2002.
43. al-Mizzī, Abū al-Ḥajjāj Yūsuf b. Zakī 'Abd al-Raḥmān b. Yūsuf (654-742/1256-1341), *Tahdhīb al-Kamāl*, Beirut, Lebanon: Mu'assisa al-Risāla, 1400/1980.

SĪRA

44. al-Bayhaqī, Abū Bakr Aḥmad b. al-Ḥusayn (384-458/994-1066), *Dalā'il al-Nubuwwa*, Beirut, Lebanon: Dār al-Kutub al-'Ilmiyya, 2nd ed. 1423/2002.
45. Ibn Hishām, Abū Muḥammad 'Abd al-Malik (d. 213/828), *al-Sīra al-Nabawiyya*, Damascus, Syria: Dār al-Kalim al-Ṭayyab, 1st ed. 1420/1999.
46. Ibn Hishām, Abū Muḥammad 'Abd al-Malik (d. 213/828), *al-Sīra al-Nabawiyya*, Beirut, Lebanon: Dār al-Jīl, 1st ed. 1411.
47. al-Qasṭallānī, Abū al-'Abbās Aḥmad b. Muḥammad b. Abī Bakr b. 'Abd al-Malik (851-923/1448-1517), *al-Mawāhib al-Laduniyya bi al-Minḥ al-Muḥammadiyya*, Beirut, Lebanon: al-Maktab al-Islamī, 1412/1991.
48. Ibn al-Qayyim, Abū 'Abd Allāh Muḥammad b. Abū Bakr Ayyū al-Zara'ī al-Jawziyya (691-751/1292-1350), *Zād al-Ma'ād*, Beirut, Lebanon: Mu'assisa al-Risāla, 8th ed. 1405/1985.

49. Ibn Sa'd, Abū 'Abd Allāh Muḥammad (168-230/784-845), *al-Ṭabaqāt al-Kubrā*, Beirut, Lebanon: Dār Beirut li al-Ṭabā'at wa al-Nashr, 1398/1978.
50. al-Ṣāliḥī, Muḥammad b. Yūsuf al-Shāmī (d. 942/1536), *Subul al-Hudā wa al-Rishād*, Beirut, Lebanon: Dār al-Kutub al-'Ilmiyya, 1414/1993.
51. Ibn Sayyid al-Nās, Abū al-Fatḥ Muḥammad (671-734 AH), *'Uyūn al-Athar fī Funūn al-Maghāzī wa al-Shamā'il wa al-Siyar*, Beirut, Lebanon: Dār al-Qalam, 1414/1993.
52. al-Suhaylī, Abū al-Qāsim 'Abd al-Raḥmān b. 'Abd Allāh (508-581 AH), *al-Rawḍ al-Unuf*, Beirut, Lebanon: Dār al-Kutub al-'Ilmiyya, 1418/1997.
53. Ibn Taymiyya, Aḥmad b. 'Abd al-Ḥalīm b. 'Abd al-Salām al-Ḥarānī (661-728/1263-1328), *al-Ṣārim al-Maslūl*, Beirut, Lebanon, Dār Ibn Ḥazam, 1417 AH.
54. al-Zurqānī, Abū 'Abd Allāh Muḥammad b. 'Abd al-Bāqī b. Yūsuf b. Aḥmad (1055-1122/1645-1710), *Sharḥ Mawāhib al-Laduniyya*, Beirut, Lebanon: Dār al-Kutub al-'Ilmiyya, 1417/1996.

FIQH AND UṢŪL AL-FIQH

55. Ibn Ḥazm, 'Alī b. Aḥmad b. Sa'īd ibn Ḥazm al-Andalusī (383-456/993-1064), *al-Muḥallā*, Beirut, Lebanon: Dār al-Fikr, n.d.
56. Ibn Ḥazm, 'Alī ibn Aḥmad ibn Sa'īd ibn Ḥazm al-Andalusī (383-456/993-1064), *al-Muḥallā*, Beirut, Lebanon: Dār al-Āfāq al-Jadīda.
57. al-Kāsānī, Abū Bakr (d. 587 AH), *Badā'i' al-Ṣanā'i'*, Karachi, Pakistan: H. M. Sa'īd Co. 1st ed. 1328/1910.
58. al-Kāsānī, Abū Bakr (d. 587 AH), *Badā'i' al-Ṣanā'i'*, Beirut, Lebanon: Dār al-Kitab al-'Arabī, 1982 AD.

59. Ibn al-Qayyim, Abū ʿAbd Allāh Muḥammad b. Abī Bakr Ayyūb al-Zarʿī (691-751/1292-1350), *Aḥkām Ahl al-Dhimma,* Beirut, Lebanon: Dār Ibn Ḥazm, 1418/1997.
60. Ibn Qudāma, Abū Muḥammad ʿAbd Allāh b. Aḥmad al-Maqdisī (d. 620 AH), *al-Mughnī fī Fiqh al-Imām Aḥmad b. Ḥanbal al-Shaybānī,* Riyadh, Saudi Arabia: Maktaba al-Riyāḍ al-Ḥaditha, n.d.
61. Ibn Qudāma, Abū Muḥammad ʿAbd Allāh b. Aḥmad al-Maqdisī (d. 620 AH), *al-Mughnī fī Fiqh al-Imām Aḥmad b. Ḥanbal al-Shaybānī,* Beirut, Lebanon: Dār al-Fikr, 1405 AH.
62. al-Shāfiʿī, Abū ʿAbd Allāh Muḥammad b. Idrīs (150-204/767-819), *al-Umm*, Beirut, Lebanon: Dār al-Maʿrifa, 2nd ed. 1406/1986.
63. al-Shaybānī, Abū ʿAbd Allāh Muḥammad b. al-Ḥasan (132-189 AH), *Kitāb al-Ḥujja*, Beirut, Lebanon: ʿĀlam al-Kutub, 1403 AH.
64. al-Shaybānī, Abū ʿAbd Allāh Muḥammad b. al-Ḥasan (132-189 AH), *Kitāb al-Ḥujja*, Lahore, Pakistan: Dār al-Maʿārif al-Nuʿmāniyya, n.d.
65. al-Shaybānī, Abū ʿAbd Allāh Muḥammad b. al-Ḥasan (132-189 AH), *al-Mabsūṭ*, Karachi, Pakistan: Idāra al-Qur'ān wa al-ʿUlūm, n.d.
66. al-Shawkānī, Muḥammad b. ʿAlī b. Muḥammad (1173-1250/1760-1834), *Nayl al-Awṭār*, Beirut, Lebanon: Dār al-Jīl, 1973.
67. al-Shurbīnī, al-Shaykh Muḥammad al-Khaṭīb (d. 977 AH), *Mughnī al-Muḥtāj*, Beirut, Lebanon: Dār ihyā' al-Turāth al-ʿArabī, n.d.
68. al-Ṭaḥāwī, Abū Jaʿfar Aḥmad b. Muḥammad b. Salama (229-321/853-933), *Sharḥ Maʿānī al-Āthār,* Beirut, Lebanon: Dār al-Kutub al-ʿIlmiyya, 1399 AH.

69. Abū 'Ubayd al-Qāsim b. al-Sallām (d. 224 AH), *Kitāb al-Amwāl*, Cairo, Egypt: Maktaba al-Kulliyāt al-Azhariyya, 3rd ed. 1401/1981.
70. Abū 'Ubayd al-Qāsim b. al-Sallām (d. 224 AH), *Kitāb al-Amwāl*, Beirut, Lebanon: Dār al-Fikr, 1408 AH.
71. Abū Yūsuf, Ya'qūb b. Ibrāhīm (d. 182 AH), *Kitāb al-Kharāj*, Beirut, Lebanon: Dār al-Ma'rifa, n.d.
72. Abū Yūsuf, Ya'qūb b. Ibrāhīm (d. 182 AH), *Kitāb al-Kharāj*, Lahore, Pakistan: al-Maktabat al-Islāmiyya, 1974 AD.
73. Ibn Zanjuway, Ḥamīd (251 AH), *Kitāb al-Amwāl*, Beirut, Lebanon: 'Ālim al-Kutub, 1403 AH.

TASAWWUF

74. Abū Nu'aym, Aḥmad b. 'Abd Allāh b. Aḥmad b. Isḥāq al-Aṣbahānī (336-430/948-1038), *Ḥilyat al-Awliyā' wā Ṭabaqāt al-Aṣfiyā'*, Beirut, Lebanon: Dār al-Kitāb al-'Arabī, 1405/1985.

HISTORY

75. Ibn 'Asākir, Abū al-Qāsim 'Alī b. al-Ḥasan b. Hibat Allāh b. 'Abd Allāh al-Dimashqī (499-571/1105-1176), *Tārīkh Dimashq al-Kabīr* (generally known as *Tārīkh Ibn 'Asākir)*, Beirut, Lebanon: Dār al-Fikr, 1995 AD.
76. al-Balādhurī, Aḥmad b. Yaḥyā b. Jābir b. Dāwūd (d. 289/892), *Futūḥ al-Buldān*, Beirut, Lebanon: Dār al-Kutub al-'Ilmiyya, 1403/1983.
77. al-Balādhurī, Aḥmad b. Yaḥyā b. Jābir b. Dāwūd (d. 289/892), *Futūḥ al-Buldān*, Alexandria: Dār Ibn Khaldūn, n.d.
78. Ibn al-Jawzī, Abū al-Faraj 'Abd al-Raḥmān b. 'Alī b. Muḥammad b. 'Alī b. 'Ubayd Allāh (510-579/1116-

1201), *al-Muntaẓim fī Tārīkh al Mumlūk wa al-Umam*, Beirut, Lebanon: Dār al-Kutub al-'Ilmiyya, 1409/1989.

79. Ibn Kathīr, Abū al-Fidā' Ismā'īl b. 'Umar (701-774/1301-1373), *al-Bidāya wa al-Nihāya*, Beirut, Lebanon: Dār al-Fikr, 1419/1998.
80. Ibn Kathīr, Abū al-Fidā' Ismā'īl b. 'Umar (701-774/1301-1373), *al-Bidāya wa al-Nihāya*, Beirut, Lebanon: Maktabat al-Ma'ārif, n.d.
81. Ibn Khaldūn, 'Abd al-Raḥmān b. Muḥammad al-Ḥaḍramī (732-808 AH), *al-Tārīkh* (*History*), Beirut, Lebanon: Dār al-Qalam, 1984 AD.
82. al-Khaṭīb al-Baghdādī, Abū Bakr Aḥmad b. 'Alī b. al-Thābit (393-463/1003-1071), *Tārīkh Baghdād,* Beirut, Lebanon: Dār al Kutāb al-'Ilmiyya.
83. al-Ṭabarī, Abū Ja'far b. Jarīr Muḥammad (224-310/839-923), *Tārīkh al-Umam wa al-Mulūk*, Beirut, Lebanon: Dār al-Kutub al-'Ilmiyya, 1st ed. 1424/2001.

DICTIONARIES

84. Ibn Fāris, Abū al-Ḥusayn Aḥmad b. Fāris b. Zakariyya al-Qazwīnī al-Rāzī (d. 395 AH), *Mu'jam Maqāyīs al-Lugha*, Beirut, Lebanon: Dār al-Jīl, 1420/1999.
85. Abū Manṣūr al-Azharī, Muḥammad b. Aḥmad (282-370 AH), *Tahdhīb al-Lugha*.
86. Ibn Manẓūr, Muḥammad b. Mukarram b. 'Alī b. Aḥmad b. Abī Qāsim b. Ḥabqa al-Ifrīqī (630-711/1232-1311), *Lisān al-'Arab,* Beirut, Lebanon: Dār Ṣādir.

ENGLISH BOOKS

87. Alan Brinkley, Frank Freidel, Richard Nelson Current, Harry T. Williams, *American History: A Survey*, New York, 7th Ed. 1987.

88. Cotterrell, Roger, *The Sociology of Law*, Butterworth's, London, 2nd ed. 1992.
89. *Electioneering: A Comparative Study of Continuity and Change*, Ed. by David Butler and Austin Ranney, Oxford: Clarendon Press, 1992.
90. Hart, James, *The American Presidency in Action 1789: A Study in Constitutional History*, New York: The Macmillan Company, 1948.
91. Jefferson, *Government by the People*, Prentice Hall, 15th ed. 1993.
92. Jolliffe, J. E. A., *The Constitutional History of Medieval England from the English Settlement to 1485.*
93. Knappen, M. M., *Constitutional and Legal History of England*, New York: Harcourt Brace, 1942.
94. Melvin I. Urofsky, Paul Finkelman, *A March of Liberty: A Constitutional History of the United States*, Oxford University Press, 2002.
95. *Selected Documents of English Constitutional History*, Ed. By George Burton Adams & H. Morse Stephens, London: Macmillan & Co. Ltd., 1901.

ABOUT THE SHAYKH

SHAYKH-UL-ISLAM DR. MUHAMMAD TAHIR-UL-QADRI is a former professor of law, an internationally renowned figure, and a learned authority in multiple fields of Islamic scholarship and contemporary academia. He authored 1000 works in 25 years, 450 of which have been published. And has delivered over 6000 recorded lectures (in English, Arabic, and Urdu) encompassing countless fields including Modern Science, Philosophy, Political Science, Economics, Law, Tafsir (Quranic Commentary), Hadith (Prophetic Traditions), Aqeedah (Creed), Fiqh (Jurisprudence), and Tasawwuf (Spirituality).

In 1981, at the head of the 14th Hijri Century, he founded Minhaj-ul-Quran International (MQI), an organization which was to spread into over 60 countries across 5 continents in a period of 25 years. MQI is a multi-dimensional organization embodying the vision of serving the needs of humanity in a comprehensive manner. It consists of: a chartered university, a research centre, a publications house, a productions house, a womens wing, a youth wing, a political wing, an international welfare foundation, an education society, an interfaith and intra-faith harmony society, and a human rights society. Amongst MQI's most notable achievements is that via. The Minhaj Education Society (MES), it established over 500 schools and colleges in a space of 25 years. MES has become one of the largest non-governmental education projects in the world. Presently, MQI has an organizational presence in 80+ countries including Canada, United Kingdom, France, Spain, Greece, Kuwait, India, Pakistan, South Korea, Japan, Malaysia, New Zealand, Australia, and Fiji.

He has spent over a quarter of a century travelling the globe promoting: the authentic and beatific teachings of Islam, global peace, education, multi-cultural harmony, social welfare, virtuous character, and human rights and equality.

In 2006, Shaykh-ul-Islam was one of four key-note speakers at the Muslims of Europe Conference which took place in Turkey to discuss Identity, Citizenship, and Challenges and Opportunities for European Muslims. The conference lasted two days and was attended by many leading Muslim scholars, leaders, and thinkers from over 20 countries.

Amongst his most notable works are: Irfan-ul-Quran, a masterful English translation of the Quran, Tafsir Surah al-Fatiha (7 volumes), Seerat-ur-Rasul (Prophetic Biography, 14 Volumes), Muqaddimat-us-Seerah, (2 Volumes based on the pattern of Muqaddimah Ibn-i-Khaldun) a preface to the Prophetic biography exploring the significance of studying each aspect of the Prophet's life including the legal, political, cultural, and scientific, Khatm-un-Nabuwa (900 pages) whereby the finality of Prophetood is established from 140 Quranic Verses and 350 Ahadith. These highly valuable books are the largest written works on their respective subjects in the history of Islamic scholarship. With the exception of Seerat-ur-Rasul which is the largest of its kind in the past two centuries, and Muqqadimah-us-Seerah which is the first of its kind in over 14 centuries of Islamic scholarship. Other notable works include Islamic Philosophy of Human Life, and the various books on modern Science such as the Quran on the Creation and Expansion of the Universe, The creation of Man, and Spiritualism and Magnetism.

Presently, 2 PHD's are being carried out on his works at Jamia al-Azhar University (Cairo). One on the 14 Volume Prophetic Biography with a particular emphasis on the volume on Prophetic Miracles. The other is on Irfan-ul-Quran (Shaykh-ul-Islam's English translation of the Quran).

Although he doesn't travel the globe as much as he used to; his lectures which are marked by a unique degree of oratory excellence continue to attract capacity crowds. They are also played and sometimes aired live on Satellite channels across the globe.

EARLY LIFE

Shaykh-ul-Islām was born on February 19, 1951 in the historical city of Jhang (Pakistan) as the son of the great spiritual master and intellectual of his time ash-Shaykh Dr Farīda'd-Dīn al-Qādrī. Shaykh-ul-Islam's birth was foretold to his father in a spiritual dream and so from a young age he was educated in the Islāmic and secular sciences simultaneously. Although he had already started his Islamic education under his father two years earlier, his formal classical education was initiated in Medina at the age of 12, in Madrasa al-'Ulūm ash-Shar'iyya which was situated opposite the green dome in the blessed house of Sayyidunā Abū Ayyūb al-Ansārī, the first residence of the Holy Prophet (blessings and peace be upon him) after his migration.

UNIVERSITY YEARS

In 1970, he received a First Class Honours Degree from the prestigious University of Punjab, and had simultaneously completed his Classical Islāmic Studies, having spent over ten years under the tutelage of his father and other eminent Shuyūkh of his time. He had achieved an unparalleled understanding of the classical *Islamic* sciences and the Arabic language. In 1972, he earned his MA in Islāmic Studies, smashing the university's record and being awarded its loftiest Gold Medal prize. In 1974, he received his LLB and began to practice as a lawyer in the district courts of Jhang. In 1978, he moved to Lahore to join the University of the Punjab as a lecturer in Law where he also completed his doctorate in Islāmic Law. He was a member of the Syndicate, Senate and Academic Council of the University of the Punjab, the highest executive, administrative and academic bodies of the University. Later, he was appointed as the Head of the Department for LLM in Islamic Legislation.

Then he became the youngest person ever to have been awarded a professorship in the history of the University by being appointed as Professor of Islamic Law.

A LIST OF SELECT WORKS

QUR'ANIC TAFSIR/SCIENCE OF QURANIC COMMENTARY

Total: 80 books .

- Irfan-ul-Qur'an (English & Urdu Translation of the Qur'an
- Tafsir Minhaj-ul-Qur'an
  (al-Futuhat al-Madaniyyah- 14 Volumes U.P)
- Development of Human Personality in the Light of Surah al-Fatihah
- No Coercion in religion
- Islamic Concept of Human Nature
- Qur'anic Philosophy of Da`wah

AHADITH WORKS/SCIENCE OF PROPHETIC TRADITIONS

Total: 75 books.

- Jami`-ul-Sunnah (a comprehensive compilation of 25000 Ahadith, totalling 20 volumes U.P)
- Al-A'ta fi Ma`rifat al-Mustafa (4 volume collection of 5000
- Ahadith on the subjects of the Excellence, Habits, Morals, Specialties and Miracles of the Holy Prophet on the pattern and style of 'Al-Shifa` of Qadi `Iyad)
- Hidayat-ul-Ummah ala Minhaj-il-Qur'an was-Sunnah (2 volumes-another collection of 3000 Ahadith)
- Al-Qawl Al-Qawi (A book on the science of Hadith
  in the Arabic language)

- Al-Khutbat-us-Sadidah (A brief textbook on the science of Hadith in the Arabic language)
- Imam Abu-Hanifah: Imam-ul-A'immah fil-Hadith (4 Volumes)

AQEEDAH/BELIEF/CREED/THEOLOGY

Total: 100 books.

- Majmu`at-ul-`Aqa'id (25 Volumes- An unprecedented compendium on Islamic Faith and Theology)
- Kitab-ut-Tawhid (a detailed treatise on the concept of the unity of Allah (s.w.t) amounting to 2 volumes)
- Kitab-ur-Risalah (2 Volumes- a detailed treatise on the excellence of Prophethood and highly esteemed station of the holy Prophet (s.a.w)
- Kitab-us-Sunnah (2 volumes- a comprehensive treatise on the authority, science and compilation of Hadith and Sunnah)
- Kitab-ul-Bid'ah (a comprehensive work on the concept of 'innovations' in Islam)

SEERAH/PROPHETIC BIOGRAPHY

- Dala'il al-Barakat (5000 styles of slaat on the Holy Prophet (s.a.w)- a masterpiece of Arabic literature, written in the style of the well-read
- Dala'il al-Khayrat of Imam Jazuli)
- Political Aspect of the Prophet's Sirah
- Economic Aspect of the Prophet's Sirah
- Administrative Aspect of the Prophet's Sirah
- Constitutional Aspect of the Prophet's Sirah
- Scientific Aspect of the Prophet's Sirah
- Cultural Aspect of the Prophet's Sirah
- Historical Aspect of the Prophet's Sirah
- Aspect of Human Rights in the Prophet's Sirah
- Aspect of Peace and Integration in the Prophet's Sirah

- Diplomatic Relations in the Prophet's Sirah
- Non-Muslim Relations in the Prophet's Sirah
- Revolutionary Struggle of the Prophet's Life

FIQH/ JURISPRUDENCE/LAW

Total: 60 books.

- Islamic Penal System and Philosophy (Shaykh-ul-Islam's PhD thesis)
- Islamic Concept of Law
- Islamic Concept of Crime
- A Comparative Study of Islamic and Western Concepts of Law
- Legal Character of Islamic Punishments
- Philosophy of Ijtihad and the Modern World
- Islam and Human Rights
- Islamic Concept of State
- Concept of Jail and Imprisonment in Islam

ISLAMIC POLITICAL AND ECONOMIC SYSTEMS

- The Constitution of Medina (A detailed exposition of the first ever written constitution in human history)
- Khilafah and Democracy (A voluminous work on the subject of the Islamic Political System)
- Islamic Economic System, its Origin and Development
- Islamic Economy and Interest free Banking
- Qur'anic Philosophy of Rise and fall of the Nations
- Nizam-ul-Mustafa: A Message and Struggle for Change

TASAWWUF

Total: 50 books.

- Reality of Tasawwuf
- Practical Code of Spirituality

- Purification of Heart and Soul
- Illness of the Heart and its cure
- Our Real Homeland
- Sin and Repentance
- Qur'anic Categorization of People
- Life –A War between Good and Evil
- Morality of Prophets
- The Awliya: Companies and Narrations

HUMAN RIGHTS

- Islam on fundamental Rights
- Islam on the Rights of Children
- Islam on the Rights of Women
- Islam on the Rights of Senior Citizens
- Islam on the Rights of Non-Muslims
- Islam on the Rights of the Disabled

MODERN SCIENCES

- Islam and Science
- Islam and Modern Medicine
- Islam and Embryology (Creation and Evolution of Man)
- Islam on Prevention of Heart Diseases
- Issues of the Modern Age and their Solutions

SELECT CHAINS OF AUTHORITY (ISNĀD)

Shaykh-ul-Islām is one of the great authentic transmitters of the Prophet's (blessings and peace be upon him) knowledge to the Umma from whom scholars of East and West, both Arab and non-Arab, have derived benefit, who come to him to receive ijāzāt (permission) and isnād (authority) as an

Imām of 'ilm in this century. He is the one who received his permission and authority from the greatest scholars of their time, and he delivers his permission and authority to hundreds of great scholars of his time. Being the author of one thousand books and a transmitter of the Holy Prophet's (blessings and peace be upon him) knowledge through five thousand orations and narrations, he has revived numerous Islāmic sciences, including 'ulūm al-Qur'ān, 'ulūm al-hadīth, 'ilm al-fiqh, al-'aqīda, at-tasawwuf, and ideology through his reconstructive efforts of Islāmic thought and philosophy in the modern age. He has more than 150 Chains of Authority contained in two of his own Thabats (Reference books on his chains of Authority) namely:

I. *Al-Jawahir-ul-Bahirah fi Asanid al-Tahirah*
II. *As-Subul-ul-Wahbiyyah bil Asanid al-Dhahabiyyah*

The following are some examples of his links to the renowned classical scholars via only one teacher:

- He is linked to al-Imam Yusuf bin Isma'il an-Nabhani directly via only one teacher, his student ash-Shaykh Husayn bin Ahmad Al-`Usayran (Lebanon).

- He is linked to al-Imam Imdadullah al-Muhajir al-Makki via only one teacher, his khalifa ash-Shaykh as-Sayyid Abdul-Ma`bud al-Jilani al-Madani (who died aged 165)

- Shaykh-ul-Islam is linked to Imam-ul-Hind Shah Ahmad Rida Khan al-Barelawi via only one teacher through three different routes:

  I. Ash-Shaykh Al-Mu`ammar Mawlana Diya'uddin Ahmad al-Qadri al-Madani > Imam-ul-Hind Shah Ahmad Rida Khan

  II. Ash-Shaykh as-Sayyid Abul-Barakat Ahmad al-Qadri al-Alwari > Imam-ul-Hind Shah Ahmad Rida Khan

III. Ash-Shaykh Al-Mu`ammar As-Sayyid `Abdul-Ma`bud al-Jilani al-Madani > Imam-ul-Hind Shah Ahmad Rida Khan

Shaykh-ul-Islam has gathered together the various fields of Classical Islamic knowledge especially the knowledge and authorities of hadith from famous centres of Islamic learning across the globe:

AUTHORITIES OF THE GREAT SHUYUKH OF MAKKAH AND MEDINA

- Al-Imam `Umar ibn Hamdan al-Mahrasi
- Al-Imam Muhammad bin `Ali bin Zahir al-Watri
- Al-Imam Ahmad bin Isma`il al-Barzanji
- Al-Imam Ahmad Sharif bin Muhammad as-Sanusi al-Madani
- Al-Imam Ahmad bin Zayni ad-Dahlan
- Ash-Shaykah Amat-ullah bint al-Imam Abdul-Ghani al-
- Muhaddith ad-Dehlawi al-Madani

Shaykh-ul-Islam receives the authorities of the above mentioned through:

- Muhhadith–ul-Haram ash-Shaykh `Alawi bin `Abbas al-Maliki al-Makki (father of ash-Shaykh as-Sayyid Muhammad bin `Alawi al-Maliki) (He had Sama' from him in 1963)
- Ash-Shaykh al-Mu`ammar Diya'uddin Ahmad al-Qadri al-Madani (Died at the age of more than 100 years)
- Ash-Shaykh Husayn bin Ahmad al-`Usayran (Lebanon- died at the age of 100 years)
- Ash-Shaykh Dr Fariduddin al-Qadri (father of Sayyidi Shaykh-ul-Islam)

AUTHORITIES OF THE GREAT SHUYUKH OF BAGHDAD

- Al-Imam `Abdur-Rahman bin `Ali an-Naqib al-Baghdadi – (Imam-ul-Awlia and Hujjat-ul-muhaddithin of his era)
- Al-Imam `Abdus-Salam al-Muhaddith al-Afandi al-Baghdadi
- Al-Imam `Abdur-Razzaq al-Bazzaz al-Muhaddith al-Baghdadi back to al-Imam as-Sayyid Mahmud ibn `Abdullah al-Alusi (author of Tafsir Ruh-ul-ma`ani)

Shaykh-ul-Islam receives the authorities of the above mentioned through:

- Ash-Shaykh as-Sayyid Tahir `Ala'uddin al-Jilani al-Baghdadi al-Afandi
- Ash-Shaykh as-Sayyid `Alawi bin `Abbas al-Maliki al-Makki
- Ash-Shaykh as-Sayyid Abdul Ma`bud al-Jilani-al-Madani
- Ash-Shaykh Dr Fariduddin al-Qadri

AUTHORITIES OF THE GREAT SHUYUKH OF SHAAM (SYRIA)

- Muhaddith ash-Sham al-Imam Muhammad bin Ja`far al-Kittani
- Muhaddith ash-Sham al-Imam Muhammad Badruddin bin Yusuf al-Hasani
- Al-Imam `Abdul-Hayy bin `Abdul-Kabir al-Muhaddith al-Kittani
- Al-Imam Abul-Makarim Muhammad Amin as-Suwayd ad-Dimashqi

Shaykh-ul-Islam receives the authorities of the above mentioned through:

- Ash-Shaykh Husayn bin Ahmad al-`Usayran (Lebanon)
- Ash-Shaykh as-Sayyid Muhammad al-Fatih bin Muhammad al-Makki al-Kittânî (Damascus)
- Ash-Shaykh Dr. Fariduddin al-Qadri

AUTHORITIES OF THE GREAT SHUYUKH OF YEMEN

- Ash-Shaykh al-Habib Hamza ibn `Umar al-Aydarus al-Habashi
- Ash-Shaykh al-Habib `Ali bin `Abdur-Rahman al-Habashi
- Ash-Shaykh `Abdul-Qadir bin Ahmad as-Saqqaf
- Ash-Shaykh `Abdullah bin Ahmad al-Haddad
- Ash-Shaykh Hasan bin Ahmad al-Ahdal al-Yamani
- Ash-Shaykh Muhammad bin Yahya al-Ahdal al-Yamani
- Ash-Shaykh Isma`il al-Yamani (author of Nafas-ur-Rahman)

Shaykh-ul-Islam receives the authorities of the above mentioned through:

- Ash-Shaykh as-Sayyid `Alawi bin `Abbas al-Maliki al-Makki
- Ash-Shaykh Muhammad bin `Alawi al-Maliki al-Makki
- Ash-Shaykh Dr. Fariduddin al-Qadri

AN UNPRECEDENTED CHAIN OF AUTHORITY

Finally, the most unprecedented, unique, highly blessed and honoured chain of authority that his Eminence Shaykh-ul-Islam possesses is through only four Shuyukh between Shaykh-ul-Islam and the Great Imams listed below:

- Sayyidina `Abdur-Razzaq bin Sayyidina al-Ghawth al-A`zam Ash-Shaykh `Abdul Qadir al-Jilani al-Hasani al-Husayni (Baghdad)
- Al-Imam Ash-Shaykh al-Akbar Muhiyy-ud-Din ibn al-`Arabi (author of al-Futuhat-ul-Makkiyyah) (Damascus)
- Al-Imam Ibn Hajar al-`Asqalani, the greatest authority on Hadith (Egypt)

His Eminence Shaykh-ul-Islam's continuous chain of authority (Isnad) up to the above mentioned Great Imams is as under:

i. Shaykh-ul-Islam narrates (with direct permission and authority) from Ash-Shaykh Husayn bin Ahmad al-`Usayran (Lebanon).

ii. He narrates from Ash-Shaykh `Abdul-Hayy bin Shaykh `Abdul-Kabir al-Kittani.

iii. He narrates from As-Shaykh al-Mu`ammar `Abdul-Hadi bin al-`Arabi al-Awwad.

iv. He narrates from al-Imam As-Sayyid `Abdul-`Aziz al-Hafid al-Habashi. (He was born in 581 (Hijra) and died in 1276 (Hijra) and lived up to 695 years (Imam `Abdul-Hayy al-Kittani, Fahras-ul-Faharis wal-ithbat, Vol.2 page 928).

v. He directly studied under and narrated from al-Imam `Abdur-Razzaq al-Jilani bin Sayyidina Ghawth-ul-Azam al-Jilani at Baghdad, from al-Imam Ash-Shaykh al-Akbar Muhiyy-ud-Din ibn al-`Arabi at Damascus and from Al-Imam ibn Hajar al-`Asqalani at Egypt.

His Eminence Shaykh-ul-Islam has received the same authority and Ijaazah of transmission from another chain:

i. His Eminence narrates from Ash-Shaykh Husayn bin Ahmad al-Usayran.

ii. He narrates from Ash-Shaykh as-Sayyid Ahmad bin Muhammad as-Sanosi al-Madani.

iii. He narrates from Ash-Shaykh as-Sayyid Muhammad bin Muhammad as-Sanosi.

iv. He narrates from Ash-Shaykh as-Sayyid Muhammad bin Ali as-Sanosi.

v. He narrates from Al-Imam Abdul Aziz al-Hafeed al-Habashi who received from all of the above mentioned three Great Imams.

SOME OF THE EMINENT STUDENTS OF SHAYKH-UL-ISLAM

The following is a selective list of some leading Islamic scholars who have received authority to transmit from Shaykh-ul-Islam.

Damascus, Syria: Ash-Shaykh As'ad Muhammad Sa`id as-Sagharji (a great scholar of `ulum-ul-Hadith and Fiqh and the author of the famous work "al-Fiqh al-Hanafi wa Adillatuhu". He is the grand imam of the renowned Jami`a Masjid al-Umawi – The Umayyad Mosque of Damascus)

Kuwait: Ash-Shaykh al-Sayyid Yusuf Hashim ar-Rifa`i (world renowned scholar and Shaykh of Tariqah)

Halab, Syria: Ash-Shaykh as Sayyid Dr. Abul-Huda al-Husayni al-Halabi

Damascus, Syria: Ash-Shaykh Abul-Khayr ash-Shukri (Khatib of Masjid al-Umawi in Damascus and head of the famous Institute of Advance Hadith Studies opened by al-Muhaddith al-Akbar Imam Badruddin al-Hasani, named Jami`-ul-Muhaddith-il-Akbar)

Baghdad, Iraq: Ash-Shaykh Dr. `Abdur-Razzaq as-Sa`di (Grand Mufti of Iraq prior to March 2003)

Baghdad, Iraq: Ash-Shaykh `Abdul-Wahhab al-Mash-hadani (famous scholar of `ulum-ul-fiqh and a renowned author)

Cairo, Egypt: Ash-Shaykh Hamdun Ahmad bin `Abdur-Rahim al-Azhari

Cairo, Egypt: Ash-Shaykh `Abdul-Muqtadir bin Muhammad Alwan al-Azhari

Cairo, Egypt: Ash-Shaykh Yusuf Yunus Ahmad `Abdur-Rahim al-Azhari

Cairo, Egypt: As-Sayyid Hamid Mahmud Ahmad Mahmud al-Azhari

Cairo, Egypt: Ash-Shaykh as-Sayyid Ahmad `Abdullah Muhammad `Abdul-Jayyid al-Azhari

Cairo, Egypt: Ash-Shaykh as-Sayyid `Abdul-Wahid Yusuf Muhammad Matawu` al-Azhari

Beirut, Lebanon: Ash-Shaykh Dr. as-Sayyid Wasim al-Habbal

Tarim, Yemen: Ash-Shaykh as-Sayyid al-Habib `Ali al-Jifri, Famous Scholar of the Arab world (U.A.E)

Tarim, Yemen: Ash-Shaykh as-Sayyid Al-Habib Salim ibn Hafiz (Hadramout)

Hyderabad, India: Ash-Shaykh Muhammad Amin ash-Sharif (Shaykh-ul-Hadith of al-Jami`a al-Nizamiya, Hyderabad, Deccan, India)

Dakka: Bangladesh: Shaykh-ul-Hadith Mawlana Habib-ur-Rahman Silhati

Glasgow, UK: Ash-Shaykh `Abdul-`Aziz Fredrick (da`i and teacher)
Sana, Yemen: Shaykh Jabrayn bin Ibrahim as-San'ani

And numerous others from many countries, including Lebanon, Syria, Egypt, Yemen, Baghdad, Sudan, Jordan, U.A.E., East Africa, India, Bangladesh and Pakistan.

For more about Shaykh-ul-Islam's life and works, his Chains of Authority, and an essay on the significance of Isnad and Ijazat for the preservation of Islamic knowledge see: *'Introducing the Life and Works of Shaykh-ul-Islam Dr Muhammad Tahir-ul-Qadri'* by Muslim Youth League UK. Also available on WWW.MINHAJ.ORG

ALSO AVAILABLE

By Shaykh-ul-Islam Dr. Muhammad Tahir-ul-Qadri

ENGLISH BOOKS

Title: Introduction to Seerah: Volume 1

Description: One of the first book's of its kind. This Introduction to the Prophet Muhammad's ﷺ Biography (Seerah) is a valuable and indispensable must-read for any person who wishes to understand the life of one of the most influential figures in history and its application and relevance in the Modern age. Built on a deep understanding of present-day requirements, it focuses on the need to study various dimensions of the Prophet's life including the intellectual, cultural, international and contemporary. Using a thematic approach, it draws upon numerous timeless wisdoms inherent in the extraordinary life of the Prophet ﷺ. In doing so, the book opens a new scholarly genre – the universal relevance of the Prophetic Biography in the complex world we live in today.

Title: Creation of Man

Description: Dr. Tahir-ul-Qadri has cogently and painstakingly established the fact that the Qur'an has systematically prefigured modern scientific research on the creation and biological development of a human-being. He has knit together evidences dispersed throughout the Qur'an to draw the conclusion endorsed by the latest scientific research. Using the inductive method employed by modern scientists, he avers the absolute superiority of the Qur'an and divine revelation on the basis of its clarity, coherence and immunity to error, contrasting it with fluctuations in human theorizing that occur over-time. The work is a reflection of thorough research and erudition in multiple Qur'anic and contemporary disciplines.

Title: Islam and Freedom of Human Will

Description: If God is omniscient then surely it means that man's destiny is pre-determined? If man's destiny is pre-determined then surely he has no freedom of human will?

This question has been one of the most prominent debates surrounding the Western study of theology in recent times. In this unique piece of academic work Shaykh-ul-Islam Dr. Muhammad Tahir-ul-Qadri expands this debate in the light of Islamic doctrine and creed. The author successfully overwhelms orientalist critics desiring to defy monotheistic faith. He also surveys how this subject occupied many Muslim schools of thought throughout history and their scholarly journeying to its explanation.

ENGLISH DVD'S

Title: Daif Hadith

Description: Regarding the science of Hadith Principles, one of the chief injustices in our time is the rejection of weak (daif) hadith. Some hold that any hadith declared weak (da'if) is condemned to rejection and has no probative value whatsoever. In this well substantiated lecture, Shaykh-ul-Islam Dr. Muhammad Tahir-ul-Qadri imparts knowledge to young Muslims clarifying their confusions concerning weak hadith. The Shaykh also explains the true status of Hadith graded Weak (Daif) according to the great

Hadith Masters (Muhadithin) of old. As usual, the style of delivery is captivating, precise, and filled with references to the works of universally accepted scholars. This easy to understand DVD contains on-screen references with multiple sources for students who wish to further their Hadith studies.

ARABIC BOOK

Title: Minhaj-us-Sawi

Description: Shaykh Dr. Muhammad Sayyid Tantawi (the Shaykh of Jamia al-Azhar University, Egypt), Shaykh Ali Jumma (Mufti of Egypt), Shaykh Dr. Ahmed Umar Hashim (former principle of Jamia al-Azhar), Shaykh Asad Muhammad Saeed as-Sagarji (Imam of Ahnaf, Syria)...the great luminaries of the age have paid their tribute to this outstanding Hadith collection declaring it a great service to the revival of the Prophetic Way (Sunnah).

The Minhaj-us-Sawi contains over 5000 hadith, all with multiple references, dealing with various topics on Belief (Aqidah), Sacred Law (Fiqh) and Spirituality (Tassawuff). Based on the compilation pattern adopted by Imam Nawawi in 'Riyadh-us-Saliheen' and Khatib Tabrayzi's 'Mishkat ul Masabih', it features novel chapter-headings relevant for today. This is a huge contribution to the present age and a prequel to a greater work yet to be published: the 25,000 Hadith collection: al-Jami as-Sunnah.

NOTES